THE TECHNIQUE
OF PREDICTION

THE TECHNIQUE OF PREDICTION

THE NEW COMPLETE SYSTEM OF SECONDARY DIRECTING

R. C. DAVISON

L. N. FOWLER & Co. Ltd.
1201/1203 High Road, Chadwell Heath,
Romford RM6 4DH, Essex

First edition June 1955
Revised edition January 1971
Reprinted 1977
Reprinted 1979
Reprinted 1983
Reprinted 1990

ISBN 085243 172 4

Printed and bound in Great Britain by
Dotesios Printers Ltd, Trowbridge, Wiltshire.

CONTENTS

PREFACE

In this volume it is my purpose to set forth a system of astrological prediction which I have developed during the course of my practical work and which I have found to be thoroughly reliable, with the added virtue that it does not entail a great deal of complicated calculation. The book has not been written for absolute beginners and presupposes a certain amount of astrological knowledge on the part of the reader.

The new system is based on the predictive technique known to astrologers as "Secondary Directions". I have extended the traditional method of Secondary Directing by adding several new methods of my own, incorporating what are usually known as "Transits" in such a way as to present them as a perfectly logical development of the original system. The traditional technique, together with its new extensions, I have christened "the New Complete System of Secondary Directing".

This system of directing, as set forth in the following pages, forms a complete and comprehensive technique of prediction. In order to present some of the new methods of progression in their proper perspective it has been necessary to restate certain fundamental astrological principles and to show how these basic principles are applied uniformly throughout the various ramifications of the system.

The ideas of many of the leading astrological writers, both past and present, too numerous to mention in detail, but to whom I gratefully pay tribute, have furnished the necessary stimuli to my efforts in building the present system, which, although it is presented here as a new and original contribution to modern astrological practice, probably embodies no feature which was not well known to our predecessors in the science in the golden days of long ago.

The student will probably find the territory covered by the first few chapters familiar to him. Later on his journey will take him along strange and long deserted thoroughfares, but he will discover every now and then that they are intersected by the broad highways of current astrological practice, of which he was already aware.

It is hoped, in a subsequent volume, to suggest a new approach to those methods of prognostication which are based on the various types of Revolutional Figures, showing not only how the main basic principles outlined in the present volume may be applied with equal effectiveness to this department of predictive technique, but also how a definite and easily recognizable link between Secondary Directions and Solar Revolutions may be established.

Chapter I

THE FOUR BASIC PRINCIPLES OF SECONDARY DIRECTING

THE basis of the predictive method expounded in this volume is the system known as Secondary or Arabian Directions, in which each day after birth is taken to represent the passage of a year of life. Some astrologers have expressed the view that Secondary Directions are unsatisfactory and do not always furnish appropriate aspects to account for the various events of life. Others have maintained that, if completely successful results are to be obtained, this method of calculating future influences must be coupled with and reinforced by a special study of the Transits in force during the period under review. Those who combine Secondary Directions with Transits usually regard the former as arising solely out of the birth chart and the latter as being completely external to the native's horoscope, representing the general conditions in the outside world. It is the object of this work to show that Transits are very intimately connected with "day for a year" directions and that they form an integral part of and are the final extension of a system of directing consisting of no fewer than four distinct time measures, each based on a common unit of time, the True Solar Day.[1]

The fundamental principle of Secondary Directions is that each day after birth represents a year of the life. Most astrologers have verified through their own experience that this symbolic measure is a valid one. Therefore it seems logical to suppose that the same time unit, the True Solar Day, can also be equated to other periods of time which, through common usage, have significance for the majority of mankind.

Those familiar with horary astrology will recall that the number of degrees that one significator is distant from an exact aspect with another may be equated, when estimating the time that a certain affair is likely to come to a head, to years, months, weeks, days or even hours, according to the nature of the event about which the inquiry is being made. For instance, when dealing with a question involving the safe delivery of a letter, it would be more appropriate to work in terms of days and weeks than in units of months and years. On the other hand, if an unattached bachelor were to inquire when he was likely to marry, it would be more logical to think in terms of months or years than in terms of days or weeks! It seemed feasible that, if one zodiacal degree could at one time represent a year and at another a month, a week or a day, there was no reason why other astrological measures, which were taken to represent a year in normal circumstances, should not also be equated to shorter periods of time in special circumstances, with equal success. Accordingly, whenever suitable opportunities occurred, experiments were made with horary

[1] An explanation of the difference between the True Solar Day, the Mean Solar Day, and the Sidereal day is given in Chapter II.

charts, using the unit of one day to represent the passage of a month or a week. The results produced by these methods were so striking that it was decided to test out the same system in natal astrology without further delay. Extensive experiments proved the worth of the two measures and led to the formulation of the complete system which is now presented for the first time in the following pages.

If we accept the hypothesis that the passage of one day after birth may equally well represent a year, a month or a week, there is no reason why we should not follow this development to its logical conclusion and equate this symbolic measure of time to its own actual period of twenty-four hours. This is, of course, nothing more nor less than the transit system which is widely used in present day astrology, with the important exception that planetary positions during the years before birth are also taken into consideration, as we shall explain later. By arriving at the transit measure by this process, however, we have shown that Transits are an integral part of Secondary Directions, being a logical extension and development of the basic idea underlying the system and not a process external to this particular directional technique.

This, then, is the first principle of the system presented in the chapters which follow. The basic period of the True Solar Day can be taken to represent four separate and distinct periods of time: a year, a month, a week or a day. For convenience of reference, these four measures will henceforward be termed the Yearly, Monthly, Weekly and Daily Series of Secondary Directions or, more simply, the Yearly, Monthly, Weekly and Daily progressions. There appears to be no logical reason why the same time unit should not also be equated, if so desired, to an hour, a minute or a second but, since this would necessitate the calculation of planetary positions for some hundreds of years ahead in order to achieve a comparatively minor refinement of timing, it does not appear worth while to employ such measures in everyday practice.

Owing to the rapidity with which the transit aspects of the faster moving planets form and dissolve, it is often unsafe to rely solely upon Transits to determine when a major event denoted by the Yearly Series of Secondary Directions is due. By bringing into play the Monthly and Weekly progressions, simplification of judgment is greatly facilitated, not only in the matter of timing major events but also in gauging the less important undertones which are liable to colour the experiences over any given period. While the influences denoted by each of these time measures will have their own separate effect, it must be remembered that, the faster the measure of time, the more transitory will be the effects of the various progressed aspects formed. Thus the passage of Venus over the radical Ascendant in the Daily progressions will rarely mark anything more than a day pleasantly spent in congenial company, or a visit to the theatre or some other form of Venusian activity. If, however, Venus arrives at the radical Ascendant by the "day for a year" measure, a major event such as marriage is likely to occur if the native is of a suitable age or, if he is already married, he may become a father. When Venus arrives at the conjunction of the radical Ascendant by the two intermediate measures, noticeable improvements in the general situation of the native will occur, provided that Venus is not attacked by the malefics at the same time, or that other stronger malefic configurations do not counteract the benefic influences. If, however, prominent Venusian directions in the Yearly Series indicate a strong possibility of marriage taking place during the year, any strong accentuation of Venus contacts in the Monthly and Weekly Series will generally serve to determine the period when the yearly direction will operate at maximum strength. Detailed examples of the manner in which directions formed by the various measures may be correlated and judgments formed upon them will be given in subsequent chapters.

It is now necessary to introduce the second fundamental principle on which the Secondary system of directing is based. The Alan Leo textbooks and many who followed along the lines laid down by the Leo school have established the idea that not only do the planetary positions on the days *after* birth bear a relationship to the subsequent events of the life, but also that the planetary positions on the days prior to the day of birth have an equally important bearing upon the life of the native. Many students find it difficult to accept the idea that planetary aspects formed in the heavens on the days before birth should have any influence on the future of the native. It should be remembered, however, that comparatively little is known at the moment of the mysteries of time and of the true significance of "past", "present" and "future". The "present" as we know it is a point ever moving forward in time which separates the "past" from the "future". Any given moment in time is merely a balancing point between time past and time to come. It must be apparent that the future pattern of events is largely conditioned by happenings which have gone before. At no point in time can we start with a completely clean sheet unconditioned by past deeds, experiences and environments. The environment into which we are born, the customs of the country and the racial habits and outlook which all of us assimilate to a greater or lesser degree, are all a legacy from the past, built up slowly but surely over hundreds of years. If we accept, as many astrologers do, the principle of continuous individual existence, either in a chain of earthly incarnations or on other planes of awareness, it follows that our birth in a physical body is not such a fortuitous happening as it may appear to be but is, in reality, the logical and inevitable outcome of all our previous actions and experiences.

The question of Fate versus Freewill has exercised the minds of many seekers after Truth throughout the ages. The law of Karma teaches that our future is largely the result of our past thoughts and actions. "As ye sow, so shall ye reap" is an axiom appreciated by all students of occultism. Yet, although much of our future may be pre-determined by our own past actions, many of which were doubtless made of our own free-will at the time, we can still exercise our free-will to govern our reactions to the situations in which we find ourselves here and now as the result of causes set in motion in the past; and occasionally we have the opportunity to mould present circumstances in accordance with our own choice.

It seems fairly reasonable to assume that planetary positions on the days after birth represent the opportunities afforded to us to choose our own future and to modify the effects of our Karma, while planetary positions on the days prior to birth are closely involved with our past and indicate the extent to which we are bound and pre-conditioned by forces set in motion through our exercise of free-will in previous existences. In order to estimate the extent to which the native will be able to modify his Karma by the exercise of will and the performance of right action at any particular period in the life, the testimonies of the planetary positions before birth must be carefully compared with and balanced against the indications given by the planetary positions after birth. Thus the complete system of Secondary directing must take into account not only the relationship which the progressed and converse planetary positions bear to the radical planets and angles but also the inter-relationship between the progressed and converse planetary positions themselves. This principle holds good not only in the case of the Yearly Series of Secondary Directions but also in the case of the Monthly, Weekly and Daily Series. The method of correlation of the progressed, converse and radical charts will be fully dealt with in the separate chapters devoted to the interpretation of directions based on each time measure. For the sake of convenience the term "progressed" directions will henceforward be used to cover both progressed and converse directions except where otherwise stated.

The third basic principle is that the Medium Coeli-Imum Coeli and Ascendant-Descendant axes of the chart are the key-points in determining the nature and timing of future events. Through these key-points are discharged the accumulated power of the radical and progressed planets at the time when exact aspects are formed between either the moving planet and the radical angle or between the moving angle and the radical or moving planet. It is fatal to consider the horoscope as static. Although the birth chart represents a definite charge of power generated at a particular moment of time, the chart itself must be considered as a living entity, continually spinning and whirling, modifying itself and unfolding its inner potentialities both through the forward and backward motion of the angles in space, and through the daily motion of the planets in the heavens before and after birth.

The fourth basic principle concerns the yearly rate at which the angles of the radical chart should be progressed, a matter over which much controversy has existed in the past. Some astrologers have borrowed the measure often used in Primary Directions and attributed to Ptolemy—the passage of one degree of Right Ascension over the Midheaven for each year of life—while others have used the measure devised by Valentine Naibod—59′ 8″, which represents the mean daily motion of the Sun. Others calculate the progressed chart as if the native were born again at exactly the same time on the days prior to and subsequent to birth, some using the Equation of Time[1] to adjust their calculations, others not. Yet another method is to add (and subtract) from the radical Midheaven one zodiacal degree for each year after birth. A variation of this method, employed by Simmonite,[2] is to add to the Midheaven the amount of arc traversed each day by the Sun on its passage through the Zodiac. Extensive experimentation with these various methods has convinced me that, in all the ramifications of Secondary directing, the best results are obtained with Simmonite's measure. Indeed, as the whole system of

[1] See Chapter II.
[2] This method was first published by Antonio Francis de Bonattis in 1617.

progressions is based on the daily motion of the Earth in relation to the Sun, it seems only logical that the apparent motion[1] of the Sun in the Zodiac should be the determining factor in calculating the progress of the most important single point in the horoscope, the Midheaven. This amount of arc, which will naturally vary according to whether the Sun is moving quickly or slowly in the Zodiac, is added to or subtracted from the radical Midheaven in order to obtain the progressed or converse positions of the angles for each separate series of progressions, whether they be yearly, monthly, weekly or daily. Full details of the methods of calculation and interpretation will be given in the separate chapters dealing with each measure of progression.

Briefly then, these are the main features of the new complete system of Secondary Directions outlined above.

1. One single unit of time—the True Solar Day—can be equated not only to a year, but to a month, a week or a day. These four types of direction are not to be regarded separately but, taken together, they form a completely integrated whole.

2. Progressions are equally valid whether measured forward or backward in time from the day of birth.

3. The angles of the birth chart rotate at a rate equal to the speed of the Sun's progress through the Zodiac on the days immediately following and prior to the day of birth.

4. The angles of the chart, both progressed and radical, are the most sensitive points and their position is of paramount importance in determining both the timing of events and their nature.

---

[1] See Chapter II.

Chapter II

SECONDARY DIRECTIONS—THEORY AND CALCULATION

THE study of astrology is largely a study of symbology. There is a special significance attaching to every horoscopical factor. Each planet, sign and aspect, each house and quadrant of the horoscope has a particular root meaning and represents a natural principle, the working out of which can be traced in the manifold activities of everyday life. There is, for instance, a meaning underlying the fact that one planet is elevated above all the others in the heavens at a particular moment of time or that one planet is placed between two others, or is the sole occupant of one hemisphere of the horoscope. The appearance and behaviour of the planets and their actual astronomical motions also have a special significance for the astrologer. Mercury, for example, is the nearest known planet to the Sun and revolves around the Sun four times in the space of just under a year. On account of his proximity to the Sun and his rapid motion, Mercury plays the role of celestial interpreter and messenger to the rest of the solar system, modifying and translating the rays of the Solar Logos for their benefit. Consequently, Mercury represents symbolically the power of intelligence and the faculty of self-expression, two factors which help to make possible the adaptation of each individual to his environment.

Our planetary system consists of one great central fixed star, the Sun, around which the planets revolve in their orbits at varying speeds. From the point of view of an observer standing on one of these planets the Sun will appear to be the moving body and will consequently seem to make a complete circuit of the Zodiac while actually the planet is travelling once round the Sun. This passage, or apparent passage, of the Sun through the twelve signs of the Zodiac is a symbolic equivalent of one whole cycle of experience. Because we are concerned solely with their effects on this planet, we on the Earth base our astrology on the apparent motion of the Sun and the actual motion of the planets in relation to our own planet. It takes the earth just over 365 days to complete one orbital revolution round the Sun. This, then, for us on Earth, is a symbolic period of time which represents one complete cycle of experience. There is, however, a faster motion of the Earth which also involves a circuit of the Zodiac.

This motion is the rotation of the Earth on its axis once every twenty-four hours. This rotary movement makes the Sun appear to travel once round the Earth every day and produces the phenomena of daylight and darkness except at the Poles. If an observer standing on the Earth's equator were to gaze for a whole day without ceasing at the point immediately above him he would have witnessed the passage of the whole Zodiac over his head during the space of his twenty-four hour vigil. It will therefore be appreciated that through the axial rotation of the Earth another kind of zodiacal circuit is completed. This circuit, although completed in a much shorter space of time, can also be regarded as symbolizing one complete cycle of experience.

It is a law of nature that the microcosm reflects the macrocosm. This is summed up in the Hermetic axiom, "As above, so below". For this reason it is possible, when two cycles of time are closely related to each other, to regard the lesser cycle as containing within itself the potentialities of the greater. This is why it is valid to equate the time taken by the Earth to rotate once on its axis, i.e., one day, to the time taken by the Earth to make one complete circuit of its orbit, i.e., one year.

Those astrological students not well versed in astronomy may feel some doubt as to which particular "day" it is that is used in this equation. Once the relative positions of the Sun, planets and fixed stars are appreciated and a degree of familiarity is obtained with the terms used in the Ephemeris, some confusion is apt to arise as to the precise difference between the True Solar Day, the Mean Solar Day and the Sidereal Day. It may not be out of place therefore, to devote a paragraph to the explanation of these three different ways of measuring the passage of a day.

The Sidereal Day is the length of time taken by the Earth to make one complete rotation on its axis measured in relation to the fixed stars. The word "Sidereal" is derived from the Latin "sidus" (genitive—"sideris") meaning "a star". While the Earth is rotating, however, it is also moving forward on its yearly journey round the Sun. In order to make one complete rotation in relation to the Sun it has, therefore, to turn a short distance farther on its axis in order that the same point on its surface may once again face the Sun at the end of each twenty-four hours. The length of time taken by the Earth to complete one axial rotation in relation to the fixed stars is approximately 23 hours 56 minutes. This is the length of the Sidereal Day. The length of time taken by the Earth to complete one axial rotation in relation to the Sun is variable. It varies, firstly, because the Earth travels round the Sun in an elliptical orbit, which means that the Earth is closer to the Sun at some seasons of the year than at others, and secondly, because the ecliptic is inclined at an angle to the equator, which means that it is not possible to divide up the quadrants of the ecliptic in proportions which correspond exactly with similar divisions of the quadrants of the equator. For everyday purposes it is convenient to use the average length of the Solar Day as a standard for measuring clock time. This twenty-four hour day is known as the Mean Solar Day. The True Solar Day is never more than sixteen minutes longer or shorter than twenty-four hours and is the time measured on the sun-dial. The difference in time between the True Solar Day and the Mean Solar Day is the reason why the Sun is rarely exactly overhead at Noon, local mean time. This phenomenon only occurs on fourteen occasions during the year, at which times the length of the True Solar Day coincides exactly with the length of the Mean Solar Day. A set of tables for each day of the year showing the number of minutes difference between the length of the Mean Solar Day and the True Solar Day is published in the Nautical Almanac. This set of Tables is known as the "Equation of Time".

From the foregoing explanation it will be appreciated that the only "day" which corresponds to a complete axial rotation of the Earth in relation to the Sun is the

True Solar Day. It is, therefore, this unit of time which should properly be equated to the longer cyclic period of one year. For all practical purposes, however, as we shall show below, it is sufficient when making calculations to use the approximate measure of one Mean Solar Day. This substitution causes a negligible inaccuracy to arise in the calculations and has the virtue of greatly simplifying operations.

The system of Secondary Directions has enjoyed a considerable vogue on account of the comparative ease with which the necessary calculations can be made. The computation of Primary Directions, on the other hand, requires the application of trigonometrical formulae. The necessary operations, though not complicated in themselves, entail a certain amount of tedious labour on the part of the calculator. All that is necessary under the system of Secondary Directions is to count as many days from the day of birth as the native is years old and then tabulate the exact aspects formed between the planetary positions in the birth chart and the planetary positions on the day so obtained. These will be the directions in force during that particular year. As has been explained in Chapter I, the count from the day of birth should be made both forward and backward in the calendar. The very simplicity of this procedure makes it possible to obtain a fair idea of the progressed and converse Secondary Directions from a mere inspection of the Ephemeris.

The calculation of the position of the progressed and converse Midheaven is a process only slightly more elaborate. The Midheaven of the radical chart advances through the Zodiac at the same rate as the Sun on the days after birth and moves backward through the Zodiac at the same speed as the Sun on the days before birth. In other words, the Midheaven always remains at the same zodiacal distance from the Sun whether the Sun is moving forward in the Zodiac, as it does in progressed directions, or backward, as it does in the case of converse directions. In order to find the position of the progressed and converse Midheaven, therefore, it is only necessary to find the Sun's position in the Zodiac on the day measuring to the year in question. If the progressed directions are being calculated it will be necessary to subtract the Sun's position at birth from the Sun's position on the directional day and add the amount of arc thus obtained to the radical Midheaven. If the converse directions are being calculated, the Sun's position on the directional day should be subtracted from the Sun's position at birth and the amount of arc subtracted from the radical Midheaven.

It is necessary to make two comments here. Since the variation in the Sun's rate of travel during any particular day is infinitesimal it is quite sufficient to base these calculations on the difference between the Sun's position at noon on the day of birth and at noon on the directional day. It will be observed that this is equivalent to measuring in Mean Solar Days and not True Solar Days. Although, theoretically, it is the True Solar Day which represents the passage of one year, as we have shown, it is near enough for all practical purposes to use the Mean Solar Day. The maximum possible variation in length of True Solar Days over the span of a hundred days, which is a long enough period to cover most lifetimes, is thirty-one minutes. In thirty-one minutes the Sun travels approximately one minute, sixteen seconds of arc. This is the maximum error possible by using this approximation. As it is usually quite unnecessary to calculate the Midheaven's progressed position more accurately than to the nearest quarter of a degree, it will be appreciated that the maximum discrepancy of just over a minute of arc caused by the use of the Mean Solar Day in this calculation may quite safely be ignored.

Once the progressed Midheaven has been calculated it is a simple matter to extract the Ascendant from the appropriate Tables of Houses for the latitude of the birth place.

The following example of the calculation of Secondary Directions is given by way of illustration. Ann Harding, a favourite film actress of former years, was born on 7th August, 1902, at Fort Sam Houston, Texas, (29° N47′, 95° W20′) at 9.12 p.m. G.M.T. The radical Midheaven was 27° ♍39′. It is required to calculate the directions measuring to the twenty-fourth birthday. The first step is to calculate the position of the progressed Midheaven in this manner:—

Day of birth..7th August, 1902.
Twenty-four days after birth measures to..................31st August, 1902.
Sun's position at noon on 31st August, 1902..................... 7° ♍ 08′
Sun's position at noon on day of birth...........................14° ♌ 02′

Difference ....23°   06′

Position of radical Midheaven....................................27° ♍ 39′
Add difference between Sun positions.............................23°   06′

Position of progressed Midheaven..............................20° ♎ 45′

By referring to the Tables of Houses for 29° N47′ we find that the Ascendant corresponding to this Midheaven is .... 4° ♑ 26′

The converse Midheaven is now calculated as follows:—

Twenty-four days before birth measures to..................14th July, 1902.
Sun's position at noon on day of birth..........................14° ♌ 02′
Sun's position at noon on 14th July, 1902.......................21° ♋ 05′

Difference ....22°   57′

Position of radical Midheaven....................................27° ♍ 39′
Subtract difference between Sun positions.......................22°   57′

Position of converse Midheaven............................... 4° ♍ 42′

By referring to the Tables of Houses for 29° N47′ we find that the Ascendant corresponding to this Midheaven is ....27° ♏ 07′

The next step is to observe whether the progressed and converse Midheaven and Ascendant are within a degree of an exact aspect with any planet in the nativity.

In this respect it is equally necessary to take into consideration the semi-sextile, semi-square, sesquiquadrate and quincunx aspects as well as the conjunction, sextile, square, trine and opposition. It will be seen that the following aspect is the only one formed between the two sets of positions:—

Asc. con. ⬜ ♂ r.

It is now necessary to tabulate any aspects formed between the planets on 31st August, 1902, and 14th July, 1902, and the Midheaven and Ascendant of the natal figure, the ascending degree of which is 15° ♐ 09′.

The progressed planetary positions can either be calculated for the same time of day as that at which the native was born, in which case the positions will measure to the birthday, or the planets' places at noon can be used. In this latter method (the Noon Date Method), which is explained below on page 19, the planetary positions measure to a date other than the birthday, unless the native was born at noon. The amount of each planet's daily motion which measures to a fraction of a year may easily be calculated at the rate of two hours' motion per month (see the table of lunar progressions on pages 20–21). It is unnecessary to draw up such a table for the planetary progressions as the daily motion of the planets is so much smaller than that of the Moon. It is therefore nearly always possible to make a visual estimate of the planets' positions at any time from an inspection of the noon positions.

The progressed aspects are as follows:—

♂ p. ✶ M.C. r.
♀ p. △ Asc. r.
♃ con. ✶ Asc. r.
♀ con. ☍ Asc. r. (applying).

The next operation is to list any aspectual contacts between the progressed Midheaven and Ascendant and the planets on 31st August, 1902, and 14th July, 1902. The following is the only aspect formed:—

☉ con. ⬜ M.C. p.

The last series of Angular Directions comprises any aspects formed between the converse Midheaven and Ascendant and the planets on 31st August, 1902, and 14th July, 1902. The following is the only aspect formed:—

♂ p. △ Asc. con.

The Solar Directions should now be calculated and tabulated in the same sequence as the directions to angles. Firstly, any aspects between the progressed Sun and the planets in the radical chart should be listed and then any aspects formed by the radical Sun and the progressed and converse planets. The final step is to tabulate the aspects formed between the progressed Sun and the progressed and converse planets, and between the converse Sun and the same planets. The following are the Solar Directions measuring to the twenty-fourth birthday:—

$\odot$ p. $\vee$ ☽ r.
$\female$ p. ☌ $\odot$ r.
$\jupiter$ con. $\opposition$ $\odot$ r.
$\odot$ p. $\square$ $\saturn$ p.
$\odot$ con. $\opposition$ $\saturn$ p.

Interplanetary Directions should now be tabulated in the same sequence as Solar Directions, taking one planet at a time and listing, first of all, any aspects formed between the progressed planet and the planets in the radical horoscope. Then aspects between the same planet in the radical chart and the progressed and converse planets should be noted and, finally, aspects formed between the progressed and converse planet and the other progressed and converse planets. The following are the Interplanetary Directions which measure to the twenty-fourth birthday in the example under consideration:—

$\female$ con. $\opposition$ $\uranus$ r. and p.
$\mercury$ con. $\square$ $\jupiter$ con.
$\mercury$ p. $\sextile$ $\saturn$ con.

We have now dealt with all types of progressed aspects except those formed by the progressed Moon. The average daily motion of the Moon is about twelve degrees, or one degree in every two hours. Measured at the rate of a day for a year, two hours represent one month. It will thus be apparent that the aspects made by the progressed Moon form and dissolve with comparative rapidity so that, at most, their effects are not likely to last for more than two months. As the calculation of the Moon's progressed aspects is rather more complicated than the computation of the Monthly, Weekly and Daily Series of Secondary Progressions it will be found that, in practice, refinements in the timing of Yearly Secondary Directions may more easily be obtained through the use of the three latter measures. Nevertheless, for the sake of completeness and for the benefit of those who may be reluctant to put aside an item of predictive technique which has enjoyed a measure of popularity in the past, we shall devote one or two paragraphs to the consideration of Lunar Secondaries.

In order to simplify the calculation of Lunar Secondaries it is convenient to employ a device known as the "Noon Date" method. The "Noon Date" marks off that proportion of the year which is represented by the difference in time between noon (G.M.T.) on the day of birth and the actual birth time, calculated at the rate of one day for a year. Two hours will therefore represent one month and four minutes one day. If the birth occurred before noon the number of hours and minutes elapsing between the time of birth and noon is turned into months and days, using the above mentioned rate, and the resulting number of months and days are counted forward in the calendar from the day of birth in order to arrive at the Noon Date. If the birth occurred after noon, the number of hours and minutes elapsing between noon and the time of birth is similarly equated to months and days, but this period is measured backward in the calendar from the day of birth in order to obtain the Noon Date. This date is operative in respect of progressed directions. To calculate the Noon Date in respect of converse directions the process is reversed, the same number of days being counted backward in the calendar from the day of birth if the birth occurred before noon and forward if the birth occurred after noon. These new dates may now be used as a foundation for all subsequent calculations based on the noon positions of the planets.

We will now calculate the Noon Dates for the horoscope of Ann Harding. As she was born at 9.12 p.m. G.M.T. the Noon Date for progressed directions will be earlier in the year than the day of birth, while the Noon Date for converse directions will be later in the year. In order to find out how many days earlier it is necessary to calculate that portion of a year which is represented by nine hours, twelve minutes, measured at the rate of two hours per month and four minutes per day. The number of days represented by nine hours, twelve minutes is therefore 138. One hundred and thirty-eight days measured backward from 7th August, 1902, gives 22nd March as the Noon Date for progressed directions. The same period measured forward from the 7th August gives 23rd December as the converse Noon Date.

It is now required to calculate the Lunar Directions measuring to the twenty-fourth birthday. Having obtained the Noon Date the next step is to determine the actual daily motion of the Moon on the directional day which measures to the year under consideration. This daily motion should then be divided by twelve in order to arrive at the amount of arc covered by the Moon in two hours, the period of time which is equivalent to one month. On 31st August, 1902, the progressed directional day which represents the twenty-fifth year in Ann Harding's life, the Moon's position at noon was 14° ♌ 31′ 02″. At noon on the day following the Moon's position was 28° ♌ 42′ 48″. The daily motion was therefore 14° 12′. (It is sufficient for all practical purposes to calculate the Moon's daily motion to the nearest minute of arc.) By dividing 14° 12′ by twelve we can obtain the amount of the Moon's motion in two hours, the period of time equivalent to one month. The average amount covered by the Moon in each two hour period is 1° 11′. By adding successive increments of 1° 11′ to the Moon's position at noon on 31st August, it is possible to compile a table in the following manner, showing the position of the progressed Moon and the aspects it forms for each month of the year:—

Noon Date = 22nd March

Date	*Moon's Position*	*Aspects*
22nd March, 1926	14° ♌ 31′	△ Asc. r., ☌ ☉ r., ☌ ♀ p., ☍ ♃ con.
22nd April, 1926	15° ♌ 42′	△ Asc. r., ☌ ☉ r., ⚺ ♀ r., ☍ ♃ con., ∠ ☿ con.
22nd May, 1926	16° ♌ 53′	△ ♅ r., p., ⚹ ♀ con., ∠ ♆ con.
22nd June, 1926	18° ♌ 04′	△ ♅ r., p., con., ∠ ♆ r.
22nd July, 1926	19° ♌ 15′	⚼ Asc. p., ⚹ ♀ r.
22nd August, 1926	20° ♌ 26′	⚹ M.C. p.
22nd September, 1926	21° ♌ 37′	⚹ M.C. p., ∠ ☽ r., ⚺ ☉ con., ⚻ ♄ p.
22nd October, 1926	22° ♌ 48′	⚻ ♄ r.

22nd November, 1926	23° ♌ 59′	⊼ ♄ r., con. ⊻ ☿ p.
22nd December, 1926	25° ♌ 10′	⊻ ☿ p., ⚹ ♂ con., ⊼ ♄ con.
22nd January, 1927	26° ♌ 21′	□ Asc. con., ⚹ ♂ con.
22nd February, 1927	27° ♌ 32′	⊻ M.C. r., □ Asc. con., ∠ ♂ r., ⊻ ♂ p.

A similar table should now be prepared to show the converse Lunar Directions. In this case it is necessary to subtract the monthly increment from the Moon's noon position on the converse directional day. The calculations are as follows:—

Moon's position at noon on 14th July, 1902 ....13° ♏ 03′ 52″
Moon's position at noon on 13th July, 1902 .... 1° ♏ 03′ 11″
_____

Moon's daily motion ....12° 01′
_____

Monthly increment = 1/12th of Moon's daily motion = 1° 00′

Date	Moon's Position	Aspects
23rd December, 1926	13° ♏ 04′	□ ☉ r.
23rd November, 1926	12° ♏ 04′	∠ M.C. r., △ ♂ r., □ ♃ r.
23rd October, 1926	11° ♏ 04′	⊡ ♂ con.
23rd September, 1926	10° ♏ 04′	□ ☿ r., ∠ ♀ p., ⊡ ♂ con.
23rd August, 1926	9° ♏ 04′	∠ ☿ p.
23rd July, 1926	8° ♏ 04′	⚹ ☉ p.
23rd June, 1926	7° ♏ 03′	⚹ ☽ r., ⚹ ☉ p.
23rd May, 1926	6° ♏ 03′	⚹ ☽ r., ⚹ ☉ p.
23rd April, 1926	5° ♏ 03′	⚹ M.C. con., ⚹ Asc. p., ⊡ ♀ r.
23rd March, 1926	4° ♏ 03′	⚹ M.C. con., ⚹ Asc. p., ⊡ ♀ r., △ ♆ p.
23rd February, 1926	3° ♏ 03′	∠ ♅ r., p., con., △ ♆ r., p.
23rd January, 1926	2° ♏ 03′	∠ ♅ r., p., △ ♆ r., con., ⊡ ♀ con.

In order to restore the minute which was lost in approximating one twelfth of the Moon's daily motion, the increment for the seventh month has been taken as 1° 01′.

Further reference will be made to the directions based on Ann Harding's chart in a subsequent chapter dealing with the interpretation of directions.

Chapter III

THE INTERPRETATION OF SECONDARY DIRECTIONS—
PRELIMINARY CONSIDERATIONS

THE most important series of directions are those involving the radical, progressed and converse Midheaven and Ascendant. The angles of the chart are especially sensitive points and when they become involved by aspect with a radical, progressed or converse planet, the influence of that planet temporarily becomes paramount in the life, producing effects according to the nature of the planet and its condition in the nativity. No important event in the life ever comes to pass unless a direction involving an angle of the horoscope is in force at the time. Solar directions are almost as potent as directions involving the angles.

It is possible to predict all the major events of the life by using only directions involving the angles and the Sun. Only comparatively minor happenings in the life are to be expected during a year in which no directions of this kind are formed. These minor events are often indicated by interplanetary directions, which, as a class, are less potent in their effects than the two previous series. Nevertheless, a study of the interplanetary directions in force is often a valuable aid in determining the precise field of operation of angular or Solar directions. In the event of there being no directions operative during the year involving the angles of the horoscope or the Sun, the interplanetary directions will then serve to establish the type of experiences likely to be encountered in the period under review. If an important event in the life is due to take place it will generally be signalled by more than one progressed aspect. Interplanetary directions, therefore, form a valuable part of progressional technique, if only for their importance as corroborative evidence.

Aspects formed between the progressed Moon and the radical, progressed and converse planets and angles are considerably less potent than the angular, solar and interplanetary series of progressions and are only effective while within a degree of exactitude, whether applying or separating. They have an influence of their own which, if it is not counteracted by the effects of any angular, solar or interplanetary progressions reaching their peak at the same time, can colour a period of about two months in quite a noticeable fashion. Their principal value, however, lies in the fact that they are apt to excite to action and "touch off" other directions which cast their influence over a much longer period of time. If, for instance, the progressed Jupiter is in conjunction with the radical Midheaven, and the progressed Moon passes over the Midheaven while the conjunction is still within orbs, the time indicated by the Lunar conjunction is likely to mark the climax of the period during which maximum results may be expected from the Jupiter-Midheaven conjunction. If two planets are in aspect in the progressed horoscope and the progressed Moon forms an aspect with either, it is then that the full effects of the aspect between the two planets are likely to be precipitated.

It is a useful practice to note the house and sign through which the progressed Moon is passing. The departments of life to which they correspond will then assume a more than usual prominence in the affairs of the native. The significance of house and sign position in the progressed horoscope is explained in the next chapter.

When all the aspects formed by progression during any one year have been tabulated, it is necessary to correlate them carefully and to arrange them in their probable order of potency. As already stated, directions involving the radical, progressed and converse angles are the most important, closely followed by directions formed by the progressed, converse or radical Sun. By observing the strength and prominence of the planets in the radical horoscope it is possible to determine which planets are likely to produce the most noticeable results when they become active by progression. Planets which may be considered prominent are those in the first, tenth, seventh and fourth houses, those which dispose of or are closely aspected by a large number of planets, and the ruler of the Ascendant.

Interplanetary aspects should next be listed and, finally, the lunar progressions.

It should be borne in mind when estimating the strength of various directions that progressions involving the radical positions of the planets are not necessarily stronger than progressions involving two progressed planets or two converse planets, or one progressed and one converse planet. Converse directions are certainly not weaker in their effects than progressed directions and often seem to act with greater strength. This may be due to the fact that the planetary positions before birth seem to be connected in a special way with the native's past actions and suggests that the majority of mankind is, as yet, unable to take full advantage of the opportunity to modify its Karma by right thinking and right action. Opportunities for modifying Karma are probably denoted by the planetary positions on the days after birth.

Although a new progressed Midheaven and Ascendant are derived each year from the radical chart, it is not practicable to use these points as the basis of a completely new chart. The progressed and converse horoscopes only gain their validity through their connection with the nativity, consequently when the student is attempting to assess the importance of the progressed and converse planetary positions, he should relate them to the framework of the natal chart and not to any position they may hold in relation to a new figure based on the progressed or converse Midheaven degree.

When estimating the length of time over which the influence of a direction is likely to operate, it will be sufficient to allow an orb of one degree on each side of the exact aspect between two bodies, except in the case of the Sun, where the orb may safely be extended to a degree and a half. A progressed aspect will therefore begin to operate as soon as the two planets, or the planet and angle, are within a degree of an exact aspect and the influence of the direction will continue to be felt until the faster moving planet or angle moves more than one degree away from the exact aspect.

There is one important exception to this rule. During the course of a lifetime the slower moving planets rarely move more than two or three degrees away from their positions in the natus. Often there are not more than three or four degrees between the position of the progressed Uranus and the converse Uranus and similarly with Neptune and Pluto. When this occurs the whole area becomes "blanketed" by the planet and the effects of a progressed aspect will last throughout the whole time that a directed planet throws an aspect to this area. These effects will naturally be somewhat diffused, but nevertheless unmistakeable. The faster moving planets, unless they are stationary for days at a time, cannot blanket an area in this manner.

Once the directions in force have been tabulated and set out in order of importance, it will generally be a fairly simple matter to judge whether the general trend is for good or ill. One good lunar direction cannot stem the tide of several adverse angular or solar directions, neither can one bad interplanetary direction upset a series of otherwise favourable progressions. Sometimes a cycle of favourable directions will extend over a period of years, to be followed in turn by an unfavourable cycle. The changeover period between the two cycles is then a most important and critical period. A year without strong directions forming, in the middle of a favourable cycle, will bring little which is likely to prove troublesome to the native, while a similar year occurring in the middle of an unfavourable cycle promises only a short respite from trouble. Where no strong influence shows out in the Yearly Series of Secondary Directions, the Monthly and Weekly Series may be brought increasingly into play in order to gain a greater insight into the planetary atmosphere for the year.

In many of the old textbooks all the good progressed aspects were interpreted as bringing fortunate events to pass, while bad progressed aspects were taken to be the indicators of misfortune. Although there is some underlying justification for such an attitude there are many cases where such arbitrary rules as these do not hold good. If, at birth, a planet is in trine to one of the angles of the horoscope, the period during which the progressed angle arrives at the square or opposition of this planet may be productive of much good, especially if the planet is a benefic, as its fundamental connection with the Midheaven or Ascendant is an harmonious one. On the other hand, if the planet involved in the configuration is a malefic, even a trine at birth to the Midheaven or Ascendant will scarcely protect the native from all harmful effects when the angle concerned progresses to the square or opposition of that planet. In a similar manner, if a planet in the radical chart is in square to either angle, the good which it is likely to bring when it forms a trine or sextile with that angle by progression is likely to be diminished on that account. If the planet concerned is a malefic, the progressed trine or sextile may even coincide with unpleasant events.

The strength of each planet by sign should also be taken into account, for a planet placed in a favourable sign brings more good when in good aspect and causes less harm when in bad aspect than would otherwise be the case.

The cardinal principle of prediction and the golden rule which should be remembered first, last and always is this: Nothing will come to pass that is not promised by the nativity. The possibilities latent in the birth chart must first be studied in as much detail as possible before any attempt at prediction is made. No matter how favourable the directions may be at a particular period of the life, no lasting good will arise from them unless the radical horoscope shows this probability.

Similarly, no lasting calamity should be predicted from prevailing bad directions if the whole trend of the nativity is favourable.

No major event will come to pass unheralded by a strong progressed aspect involving either the Midheaven or the Ascendant. It is safe to say also that no important happening in the life will take place unless two or three indications of the same type of event are present in the directions covering the period. The Sun will nearly always be involved in one of these progressed aspects, for the Sun represents the inner core of each chart. If an event is of real significance, therefore, it must necessarily have repercussions on the inner as well as the outer life.

It cannot be stressed too often that it is the angles of the horoscope, the Midheaven and the Ascendant and their opposite points, which are the most important factors in the whole chart. Although interplanetary aspects formed by progression are likely to have some influence on the life, their maximum effect will not be felt unless one or more of the planets involved is, at the same time, in aspect with either the radical or the progressed angles of the horoscope. These angles are the "flashpoints" through which the inner potentialities of the horoscope are externalised. If a progressed interplanetary aspect does not find an outlet through the angles of the chart its effects will not reach their maximum expression. The strongest progressed interplanetary aspects will be those formed between planets which were in aspect with each other at the moment of birth.

It often happens that in the nativity there are complexes of planets in almost exact aspect, so that the progressed angles of the chart form aspects simultaneously with several radical, and sometimes with several progressed planets at the same time. In cases such as these the full significance of these planetary complexes must be understood before any predictions can be formulated. If, for instance, Venus is in close square to Mars and Saturn in the birth chart, the arrival of the progressed Ascendant at the conjunction of the radical Venus is far more likely to bring sorrow than joy into the life.

Sometimes it will happen that a planet which was in close aspect to the Ascendant or Midheaven at birth moves through the Zodiac by progression for a number of years at the same rate as the angle with which it formed the radical aspect. The planet and angle will thus remain equidistant as they progress and will simultaneously form aspects with other radical and progressed planets. Such progressed aspects occurring simultaneously will have an added power and will operate very strongly during their period of influence.

When the angles of the chart arrive by progression at a point in the Zodiac midway between two radical planets, especially if these planets are in aspect to each other in the birth chart, events of the nature signified by the two planets are to be anticipated.

It will be apparent that as the Midheaven and Ascendant progress through the Zodiac, the intermediate house cusps will also progress. The aspects formed between progressed planets and radical house cusps and between radical planets and progressed cusps will always herald events of the nature of the house involved. These events will not be of primary importance unless directions giving similar indications involve the Midheaven or Ascendant. When the angles of the progressed horoscope reach a degree of the Zodiac held by one of the intermediate house cusps of the radical figure events of the nature of that house are likely to occur. A similar indication is given when the progressed house cusp reaches a degree held by the radical Midheaven or Ascendant. The foregoing remarks apply particularly to house cusps calculated in accordance with the system of Placidus.

When making predictions it is necessary to bear in mind that the full effect of a direction may not always immediately manifest itself. The native may inaugurate a change of course which coincides with a certain direction and he may not experience the full consequences of that change until many months, or even years, later. If the initial steps were taken under good directions the final outcome is likely to be beneficial; if under adverse directions, the result is likely to be disappointing unless in either case there are strong indications to the contrary in the nativity.

Absolute accuracy of interpretation is, in the very nature of things, not always possible to achieve, for, were astrologers able to predict the nature of events down to the very last detail, it would seem that the free will of the individual would have no bearing at all upon his destiny. It is, however, surprising how closely the astrologer can indicate the pattern of future events once he has mastered the symbology of astrology and familiarised himself with the principles and departments of life represented by the various signs, planets and houses. The student should be content, at first, to confine his predictions to general broad outlines of the trend of events and not attempt to particularise too much.

Chapter IV

THE SIGNIFICANCE OF SIGNS, HOUSES AND ASPECTS IN THE PROGRESSED HOROSCOPE

WHEN predicting, it must be remembered that the effects of a planet in the progressed horoscope depend upon the quality of the native's response to the stimulus received from that planet. The nature of this response is shown by the condition of the planet in the radical chart and is modified in each case according to the sign and house occupied by the planet and the aspects which it receives. Thus a planet in the progressed horoscope tends not only to bring events of a kind denoted by its own intrinsic nature but also experiences of a type signified by the sign and house in which it is placed at birth, and of the house or houses of which it is the ruler.

If the Sun is in the Sixth House at birth in the sign Gemini and is the ruler of the Eighth House, then, whatever sign or house it enters by progression after birth, it will affect the life mainly in terms of those things signified by the sixth and eighth houses and by the sign Gemini. Each planet will also produce effects in terms of its own essential nature, apart from the sign and house in which it is placed. It is not always easy to determine the precise field in which a progressed aspect will operate since it may at one time work out in terms of the sign occupied by the planet and at another in terms of the house tenanted by the planet or in terms of the planet's own intrinsic nature. It is not unusual for events falling within each of these three different categories to occur during the operative period of a single direction.

When estimating the effects likely to be produced by the sign and house occupied by a planet in the progressed horoscope it will be sufficient for all practical purposes to consider the implications of signs and houses as being interchangeable. The houses are a reflection of the signs and have the same basic meaning as the signs. Opposite signs of the Zodiac represent two poles of the same principle consequently the same root meaning underlies both signs. Furthermore, although planets in the first six signs and the houses below the Earth are related to the individual or interior application of the principles involved and planets in the last six signs and the houses above the Earth are related to the universal or exterior projection of these same principles upon the world at large, it will be found that it is often difficult to separate the effects of opposite houses and opposite signs, for each house and each sign is the complement of its opposite number. A planet in the natal Eighth House, therefore, is not only likely to act in much the same way as a planet in Scorpio, but may act as if it were in the natal Second House or in Taurus.

This interchangeability tends to simplify rather than to confuse interpretation and once the essential meanings of planets, signs and houses are understood it should not be difficult to get a fairly accurate picture of the various types of events likely to be expected at any given period in the life.

Besides producing effects in terms of the sign and house it occupies in the nativity, a planet will also act in terms of the house or houses over which it has rule in the radical horoscope, as well as through the sign and house into which it moves by progression.

In the paragraphs that follow, the significance of each house and the corresponding sign is outlined briefly and then each pair of houses and signs is considered together for the purpose of assessing the probable effect of directions involving planets placed in those signs or houses.

FIRST HOUSE. ARIES.

Places a focus on the native's own individual approach to the world and his immediate reaction to the problems confronting him; the energies and abilities which are ready to hand.

Corresponds to the whole physical body; the head, brain, eyes, upper jaw and the face as a whole.

SEVENTH HOUSE. LIBRA.

Places a focus on all those things which help to complete the native's experience and round off his relationship to the world at large; partners in private and in business life; those who would be our partners but for some basic misunderstanding which makes them our enemies.

Corresponds to the kidneys and lumbar region.

Directions Involving Planets in Either Sign or House :—

Bring opportunities for exercising personal initiative and enterprise, either in matters of individual self-expression (Exs. 1, 2 & 3) or in making adjustments to the partners needs; marriage (Exs. 2, 4 & 5); amicable business co-operation (Ex. 6); bringing quarrels to a peaceful end; engaging in political activities (which relate to the individual's adjustment to society and the adjustment of one branch of society to another) (Exs. 6 & 7).

Threaten danger of lawsuits (Ex. 8); open breaches; marriage troubles (Ex. 9); wars (in horoscopes of national leaders).

May lead to undertaking highly individual work of an active nature, giving scope for self-assertion and pioneering; work in connection with engineering, salesmanship, art, politics, the armed forces or the legal profession.

May affect health through neuralgia, insomnia, headache, dizziness, eye trouble, toothache, lumbago, fevers, diabetes, Bright's Disease, kidney diseases (Ex. 10), urinary troubles, nephritis.

Examples

1. Madame Blavatsky. M.C. p. ⚺ ♀ r. in ♈. Founded the Theosophical Society.
2. Colonel Lindbergh. Asc. p. ☌ mid-point ☽ ♅ r. in First House. M.C. con. △ mid-point ☽ ♅ r. in First House. Married. Made record-breaking flight to the Orient.
3. Karl Marx. Asc. con. ⚹ ♄ r. in First House. Founded a Radical newspaper.
4. Annie Besant. M.C. con. ⚹ ☿ r. in Seventh House in ♎. M.C. con. △ ♅ r. in ♈. Asc. con. ⚹ ♀ r. in ♈. Married.

5. Prince Bismarck. M.C. con. ☍ ♃ r. in ♎. M.C. p. ☍ ♅ r. in ♈. Married.
6. Annie Besant. M.C. p. △ ♀ p. in ♎. Met Bradlaugh, with whom she worked in close partnership in the political world for several years.
7. Cecil Rhodes. M.C. r. ✶ ♀ p. (♀ r. in Seventh House). Elected a member of the Cape Assembly.
8. Mary Baker Eddy. Asc. p. ☌ ♃ con. in ♈. Successfully defended a libel lawsuit.
9. Mary Baker Eddy. M.C. con. △ ♅ con. in First House. Divorce.
10. Mary Baker Eddy. Asc. con. ☍ ♀ con. and ♃ ♄ r. in ♈. Ill with renal calculi.

SECOND HOUSE. TAURUS.

Places a focus on the native's resources (material, physical, emotional, mental and spiritual) and the way in which he is able to mould them in order to consolidate his position (Ex. 1).

Corresponds to the neck, throat, tonsils, larynx, lower jaw, ears and the Thyroid Gland.

EIGHTH HOUSE. SCORPIO.

Places a focus on the native's ability to develop and reinforce his resources as a result of the impact on him of the world at large; the resources of others and the part they are likely to play in the native's life; the native's power to transmute his resources (through regeneration (Ex. 2) rebirth and, finally, death).

Corresponds to the nose, bladder, reproductive and excretory organs.

DIRECTIONS INVOLVING PLANETS IN EITHER SIGN OR HOUSE :—

Bring opportunities for improving the financial position and adding to possessions (Ex. 3); building the foundation of some enterprise (Exs. 4 & 5); increasing mental resources by analysing and probing into the physical laws of the Universe; multiplying spiritual resources by acquiring a knowledge of the secret laws underlying the Universe; achieving regeneration; undertaking study and research requiring intense application.

Threaten danger of financial losses; illness (through neglecting or foolishly expending physical resources) or death (if the body is too broken down) (Exs. 6, 7, 8 & 9); bereavement.

In extreme cases the native may act in such a way as to bring about the deaths of others.

May lead to undertaking activities to do with the exploitation of the physical resources of the earth, especially farming and mining; occupations connected with decay and death—brewer, butcher, undertaker, soldier—with the husbanding or building up of physical resources—doctor, surgeon, masseur—with hygiene—sanitary inspector, sewerman—or with scientific research; work underground (or under the sea); work in connection with building—bricklayer, decorator, engineer, architect—with finance—cashier, bank clerk—or with music (on account of the connection with the vibration of sound upon which the whole Universe is founded).

Affect health through diphtheria, laryngitis, tonsillitis, nasal polypi, throat trouble, apoplexy, quinsy, sex diseases, rupture, highly infectious diseases.

EXAMPLES

1. Karl Marx. ☉ p. ☌ ♀ r. Wrote *Das Kapital.* (Radical ☉ in Second House.)
2. Adolf Hitler. M.C. p. □ ♆ r. in the Eighth House. Asc. con. △ ♆ r. in the Eighth House. Obsessed with the idea of regenerating Germany.
3. Jay Gould. Asc. con. ☌ ♂ p. (♂ r. in ♉). Detected in fraudulent business manipulations.
4. Karl Marx. Asc. p. ☌ ☽ r. in the Second House. Founded a radical newspaper. Established home permanently in England.
5. Madame Blavatsky. Asc. con. ⚹ ☉ r. in the Second House. M.C. con. ☌ ♃ r. in the Eighth House. Founded the Theosophical Society.
6. Cecil Rhodes. Asc. con. ⚻ ♅ r. in ♉. Given six months to live by his doctor. He was then twenty.
7. Cecil Rhodes. M.C. con. ☍ ♆ r. in the Second House (applying). M.C. r. ☍ ☿ ♂ con. ☌ ♀ r. in ♉. Asc. con. ☍ ♄ con. (radical ♄ in ♉). Death.
8. Ralph Waldo Emerson. M.C. p. ☌ ♆ con. in ♏. Death.
9. Adolf Hitler. M.C. con. ☌ ♀ r. in the Eighth House. Asc. p. ☍ mid-point ♆ ♀ r. in the Eighth House. Death.

THIRD HOUSE. GEMINI.

Places a focus on the native's immediate environment and all the processes (physical and mental) by which he determines his relationship to it—all means of transport, communication, the written and the spoken word, the telephone, newspaper, wireless, television and all mediums of propaganda; neighbours, sisters and brothers (who are our neighbours in a more intimate sense); the mental powers and their unfoldment by means of primary education.

Corresponds to lungs, upper ribs, shoulders, upper arm, nervous system and the oxygenation of the blood.

NINTH HOUSE. SAGITTARIUS.

Places a focus on the world outside the native's immediate surroundings and the means by which he makes contact with it (either physically, mentally or spiritually) —long journeys, voyages, exploration; higher education—the Law, philosophy and comparative religion.

Corresponds to hips, thighs and sciatic nerves.

DIRECTIONS INVOLVING PLANETS IN EITHER SIGN OR HOUSE :—

Bring opportunities for travelling (Exs. 1, 2 & 3); improving educational standards (Exs. 4 & 5); gaining scholastic honours; engaging successfully in spreading propaganda (Ex. 6); writing and publishing books and articles (Exs. 7 & 8).

Threaten danger of accidents involving shoulders, upper arms and thighs; mishaps while travelling; interruptions in education; illness or death of brothers, sisters or neighbours.

May lead to undertaking activities in connection with transport (Ex. 9) or communications (work on a newspaper, as a Post Office or railway official or with haulage or public transport companies); as a traveller, agent or go-between; as a lawyer or judge; in connection with the dissemination of ideas (teacher (Ex. 5), lecturer, clergyman, author, publisher, journalist, publicity agent), with the tabulation of facts (secretary, clerk, typist), or with foreign countries (importer, foreign agent, explorer).

May denote events in the lives of brothers, sisters (Ex. 10) or neighbours.

Affect health through bronchial illnesses, consumption, pneumonia, pleurisy, asthma, sciatica, lumbago, rheumatism, nerve disorders, insufficient oxygenation of the blood, mental strain and mental troubles.

EXAMPLES

1. Colonel Lindbergh. M.C. con. △ ☽ r. in ♐. M.C. p. △ ☉ r. in the Third House. Asc. p. ☌ ♅ p. in ♐. Made record-breaking flight across the Atlantic.
2. Albert Einstein. Asc. con. in ♊ △ ♃ r. in the Ninth House. Emigrated to Italy.
3. Cecil Rhodes. M.C. p. ⚺ ♃ r. in ♐. M.C. con. ⚹ ♃ r. in ♐. First travelled to South Africa, where he was to make his reputation.
4. Ralph Waldo Emerson. Asc. p. ☍ ☉ r. in ♊. Entered Harvard University.
5. Ralph Waldo Emerson. Asc. p. in ♐ △ ☽ r. in the Ninth House. Graduated. Taught in brother's school for young ladies.
6. Jay Gould. Asc. r. ☌ ☿ p. (☿ r. in ♊). Acquired the *New York Times*.
7. Madame Blavatsky. M.C. p. ⚺ ☉ con. in ♊. *The Secret Doctrine* published.
8. Mary Baker Eddy. Asc. p. ☌ ♀ r. in the Third House. Founded the Christian Science Publishing Society.
9. Henry Ford. M.C. con. ☌ ☉ r. in the Ninth House. Founded the Detroit Automobile Company.
10. Mary Baker Eddy. ♀ p. △ ♃ r. (ruler of the Third House). Marriage of her sister.

FOURTH HOUSE. CANCER.

Places a focus on the native's power of assimilation (his ability to draw upon the storehouse of experience gained in the past—the extent to which he has assimilated that experience and absorbed it into the subconscious mind so that it may provide mental and emotional pabulum for the present); the parents (as a living link with the past—the flesh and blood representatives of his physical heredity); inherited property, estates; the domestic environment (where he can assimilate present experience)—in a wider sense—the homeland; the beginning and end of life (the one giving the opportunity to gather fresh experience and to make use of that previously assimilated, the other ushering in a fresh period of assimilation); the root causes underlying the native's present incarnation.

Corresponds to the stomach, breasts, diaphragm, pancreas, the upper lobes of the liver, the elbows, womb and ovaries.

TENTH HOUSE. CAPRICORN.

Places a focus on the way in which the native projects the harvest of his assimilated experiences upon the world at large—his conscious strivings to attain a chosen goal; his position in the world; the way in which he earns his living.

Corresponds to the knees, joints, bony framework of the body, hair and skin.

DIRECTIONS INVOLVING PLANETS IN EITHER SIGN OR HOUSE :—

Bring opportunities for gaining advancement (Ex. 1), honours and recognition; improving domestic conditions; opening up fresh avenues of experience (Ex. 2); undertaking additional responsibilities.

Threaten danger of damage to prestige; upsets in the career (Ex. 12) or in the domestic sphere; illness or death of a parent (Exs. 3, 4, 5 & 6); the death of the native (if other severe directions are operative—these nearly always involve the first or seventh houses and also the second or eighth houses as well).

May lead to undertaking activities in public positions or in public administration, in a Government department or in politics; in an occupation connected with the supplying of the domestic needs of the public—shopkeeper, dealer in household commodities, cook, caterer, hotelier, innkeeper, launderer or plumber; connected with land, property or trading—farmer, builder, estate agent or merchant seaman; in connection with nurturing the young or tending young growth—nursing or market gardening.

May denote events in the parents' life (especially when the native is young), a change of work or residence (Exs. 7, 8, 9, 10 & 11); inheritance of property.

Affect health through digestive ailments, catarrh, dropsy, sclerosis, skin diseases, rheumatism or chills.

EXAMPLES
1. Karl Marx. M.C. p. ☌ ♃ r. in ♑ (ruler of the Tenth House). Appointed editor of a radical newspaper.
2. Ralph Waldo Emerson. M.C. p. ☌ ♃ r. in the Tenth House. Beginning of career.
3. Adolf Hitler. M.C. p. ☌ ♄ r. in the Tenth House. Father died.
4. Prince Bismarck. M.C. p. ☍ ♅ p. in the Fourth House. Father died.
5. Madame Blavatsky. M.C. p. ☍ ☽ r. in the Fourth House. Taken into the charge of her grandmother after her mother's death.
6. Anne Morrow Lindbergh. M.C. p. ☌ ♂ p. in ♋ in the Tenth House. Father died.
7. Annie Besant. M.C. p. ☍ ☽ r. in ♋ in the Fourth House. Moved into lodgings.
8. Mary Baker Eddy. M.C. p. ☌ ♅ r. in ♑. Acquired a new residence for use as the Headquarters of the Christian Science movement.
9. Anne Morrow Lindbergh. M.C. p. ⚺ ☉ r. in ♋ in the Tenth House. Returned to the United States after several years' residence in Europe.
10. Colonel Lindbergh. M.C. r. △ ♃ con. in ♑ (ruler of the Fourth House). Returned to the United States after several years' residence in Europe.
11. Mary Baker Eddy. M.C. p. ⊼ ♄ r. in the Fourth House. Moved with her husband to a very lonely locality.
12. Albert Einstein. M.C. p. ☌ ♄ r. in the Tenth House. Unable to obtain employment.

FIFTH HOUSE. LEO.

Places a focus on the native's power of Individualisation and desire for Self-Expression—his ability to exploit the innate talent denoted by the fourth house and to add fresh accomplishments to his inherited abilities; creative abilities—the amount of power with which he is endowed or which he is able to generate; enterprises, whether material (financial speculations—emotional (love affairs)—mental (creation in the realm of art or the drama) or spiritual (faith wielded as a dynamic power) (Ex. 1); power to organize materials and order results; children (as a flesh and blood manifestation of his desire for self-expression); hobbies, holidays and all ways in which he seeks pleasure and entertainment.

Corresponds to the heart, spinal cord, the dorsal region of the spine and the forearm from below the elbow to the wrist.

ELEVENTH HOUSE. AQUARIUS.

Places a focus on native's ability to express his Individuality in the world at large; friendships—as a means of wider self-expression (he chooses his friends because they help to bring out in him those qualities that he likes to display and to develop); ideals—by means of which he may rightly direct the projection of his creative abilities upon the world at large; participation in group enterprise—for speculation or gain (business companies or corporate entities) (Ex. 2)—or for a creative purpose (societies and associations) (Exs. 1—by polarity, & 3).

Corresponds to the circulation of the blood and the leg from below the knee to the ankle.

Directions Involving Planets in Either Sign or House :—

Bring opportunities for making friends (Ex. 4); engaging in love affairs (Ex. 5); speculating successfully; realising ideals; wielding power as a result of being elevated to a high position; achieving success in the world of sport or entertainment.

Threaten danger of quarrels with friends; broken love affairs; misfortunes involving friends (Ex. 6); setbacks in speculation; reverses in sport or while seeking entertainment, or holiday-making; the illness or death of offspring (Exs. 7 & 8).

May lead to undertaking work in which he can give free rein to his creative talents or through which he can attract attention to himself—stage work or an occupation connected with public entertainment or some field of artistic endeavour (in some cases he may exercise these talents by writing or inventing); an occupation giving scope for organizing ability—as manager or head of a concern; work with a public corporation or a large undertaking (possibly the Civil Service or the Armed Forces); work connected with speculation—stockbroker, bookmaker or financial speculator; occupations connected with the use of power in all forms—particularly electrical power—and with ostentatious display—jeweller, perfumier or cosmetician.

May denote the birth of a child (Exs. 7, 9 & 11); significant events in the life of a son or daughter.

Affect health through fevers, varicose veins, nervous diseases, anaemia or cramp.

Examples

1. Madame Blavatsky. M.C. p. ⚺ ♀ r. (ruler of the Fifth House). Asc. con. ⚹ ☉ in ♌. Founded the Theosophical Society.
2. Henry Ford. M.C. p. ☌ ♃ con. (radical ♃ in the Eleventh House). Founded the Detroit Motor Company.
3. Annie Besant. M.C. p. in ♒ ⚹ ♅ r. Joined the Theosophical Society.
4. Prince Bismarck. ♀ p. in ♌ △ ♅ r. Reconciled with the Emperor after his resignation.
5. Prince Bismarck. Asc. con. in ♌ ⚹ ♃ r. (ruler of the Fifth House). Twice engaged in one year.
6. Albert Einstein. ♂ p. in ♒ □ ♀ r. in the Eleventh House. His friend Adler was sentenced to death for having assassinated the Prime Minister of Austria. He was later reprieved.
7. Colonel Lindbergh. ♀ con. ☌ ♂ r. in ♒. Baby son kidnapped and murdered. Second child born.
8. Henry Ford. ♂ p. ☌ ♃ r. in the Eleventh House. Death of son.

9. Anne Morrow Lindbergh. M.C. p. ✶ ☿ p. in ♌. Son born.
10. Jay Gould. ☉ con. ☐ ♆ r. in ♒. Daughter born.
11. Jay Gould. ♀ con. △ ☽ r. in the Fifth House. Son born.

SIXTH HOUSE. VIRGO.

Places a focus on the native's power to order and utilize his resources; his final adjustment to his own immediate environment; his efforts to achieve perfection (the technique he employs and the tools he uses in order to make the best of the materials at his disposal—whether mental, moral or physical materials); his work as a subordinate or apprentice—whether learning the essentials of a trade or whether training himself for physical or spiritual conquests (perfection can only be achieved after long and diligent practice in a subordinate role, understudying those who are more skilled and experienced); his knowledge of the laws of nature (Ex. 1) and his ability to work in conformity with them (in order to utilize the Earth's resources with the maximum efficiency)—if he cannot deal effectively with the physical or psychic materials at his disposal he becomes liable to illness.

Corresponds to the abdominal region, the large and small intestines (which aid the assimilation of nourishment and assist in the elimination of impurities); the lower lobes of the liver, the spleen, the duodenum and the hands (man's original tools).

TWELFTH HOUSE. PISCES.

Places a focus on the native's final adjustment to life as a whole; his efforts to perfect his relationship with the world at large; his knowledge and understanding of the hidden laws of nature (Ex. 2—by polarity) (the illusion of matter and of all the manifest Universe must be comprehended before the lesson of the Twelfth House can be thoroughly learned); his "Achilles' Heel"—the measure by which he falls short of achieving his purpose—his weaknesses of character which play him false in the hour of need and result in his self-undoing—his failure to make a satisfactory adjustment to life due to a lack of true perspective; under the surface conditions; secret enemies.

The Twelfth House is the house of end results. Its fruits are the harvest of the previous eleven houses. If the native can learn the lesson of Resignation to the Will of God and gladly accept the trials and tribulations of the Twelfth House as the measure of the amount by which he falls short of perfection he will accordingly shorten his apprenticeship in the school of Life.

Corresponds to the feet.

DIRECTIONS INVOLVING PLANETS IN EITHER SIGN OR HOUSE:—

Bring opportunities for gaining benefits through a sound sense of perspective; through the right use of opportunities for service; through an improved knowledge of the techniques involved in the native's day to day work; through the helpful co-operation of subordinates; through advancement to a position of subordinate authority (Ex. 8).

Threaten danger of difficulties arising from a faulty adjustment to life as a whole (physical or mental breakdown, resulting in an illness requiring hospital treatment or a long period of convalescence (Exs. 3, 4, 5 & 6) or, in extreme cases, a moral collapse which may lead to criminal activities; retarded progress through neglecting to take proper advantage of favourable opportunities, through the hampering influence of unfortunate circumstances, or through perpetually striving after the unattainable; difficulties as a result of the lack of co-operation of subordinates (Ex. 7); setbacks in his own work as a subordinate.

May lead to the undertaking of work demanding painstaking attention to detail—editor, clerk, teacher, chemist, research worker, photographer, film actor, detective; affording opportunities to serve others, particularly those who are sick physically, mentally or spiritually—nurses, doctors, workers in hospitals, prisons and institutions; connected with prepared food[1] or the manufacture or sale of clothing or footwear—grocer, food supplier, tailor, haberdasher, boot and shoe repairer, shoemaker; connected with animals—cattle dealer, veterinary surgeon; in subordinate positions, especially in the commercial world, in occupations demanding technical skill or in all kinds of "peasant industries".

May denote a period when the native's adjustment to life as a whole is tested (he may sometimes feel compelled to resign his position (Exs. 9 & 10) or he may suffer confinement in some form (Ex. 11); a change in his everyday work and an opportunity to learn fresh techniques.

Affect health through illnesses in general; constipation, diarrhoea, typhoid, enteritis, appendicitis, intestinal diseases, gout, dropsy, dyspepsia, malnutrition, an increased susceptibility to infectious diseases, foot troubles and accidents involving the hands and feet.

EXAMPLES

1. Albert Einstein. Asc. p. ⚹ ♀ p. ☍ ☽ r. in the Sixth House. Awarded the Gold Medal of the Royal Astronomical Society for his work on the Theory of Relativity.
2. Madame Blavatsky. Asc. con. ☌ ☿ con. □ ♂ ♄ r. in ♍ (radical ☿ in ♍). Wrote *The Secret Doctrine.*
3. Prince Bismarck. M.C. con. ☌ ♀ r. in ♓. Seriously ill.
4. Karl Marx. ♀ con. ☌ ♄ con. in ♓. Ill with pleurisy.
5. Cecil Rhodes. M.C. p. ⚺ ♃ r. in the Twelfth House. M.C. con. ⚹ ♃ r. in the Twelfth House. Convalescence in South Africa after his health had broken down.
6. Madame Blavatsky. M.C. p. ☌ ♄ con. (♄ r. in ♍). Ill with Bright's Disease.
7. Mary Baker Eddy. ♂ p. □ ♄ r. (♂ r. in the Sixth House). Rebellion among her followers, who objected to her dictatorial methods.
8. Prince Bismarck. ♂ r. in the Sixth House △ ♃ p. Became a Deputy in the Landtag.
9. Colonel Lindbergh. M.C. r. ⚻ ♀ con. (♀ r. in ♓). Resigned from the Air Corps of the United States Army.
10. Ralph Waldo Emerson. M.C. p. □ ♄ p. (♄ r. in ♓). Resigned his position as pastor after the death of his wife. He was deeply depressed in health and spirits.
11. Annie Besant. M.C. p. □ ♅ r. (ruler of the Twelfth House). Interned during the First World War as her activities as President of the Indian National Congress were held to be subversive.

[1] Raw food and drink—as part of the natural resources of the Earth—comes under the Second House, while prepared food and drink—which has been subjected to special processes—comes under the Sixth House.

The signs in which the progressed angles fall often afford a clue as to the nature of the events to be expected. Marriage often takes place when the progressed Midheaven in Libra forms an aspect with a radical or progressed planet and frequently long journeys are undertaken when the progressed Ascendant in Gemini is linked by aspect to a radical or progressed planet.

Although the close affinity between signs and houses in their relationship to events has been stressed above it is necessary to emphasize that the identity of the two is not so coincidental in all respects. The sign position of a planet has, for instance, a greater bearing on character than its house position, although the latter is by no means negligible, since a planet placed close to an angle of the nativity will show out more strongly in the psychology of the native than will a cadent planet.

It is much easier to discern a link between the Cardinal, Fixed and Mutable signs, which correspond to the Rajas, Tamas and Sattva of Hindu philosophy, and the Angular, Succedent and Cadent houses of the horoscope than it is to find a marked similarity between the action of the Fire, Earth, Air and Water signs and the corresponding houses. The Cardinal signs are analagous to the Angular houses of the horoscope. They are initiatory and their sphere is that of activity. The Fixed signs are comparable with the Succedent houses. They are conservative; they are the storehouses and generators of power; their role is that of building, consolidating and making permanent. They are connected with the realm of the emotions. The Mutable signs correspond to the Cadent houses. They are diffusive in their action, spreading the power derived from the fixed signs and houses and acting as a communicating link between the Cardinal and Fixed Principles. Their domain is that of the intellect.

The connection between the elements Fire, Earth, Air and Water and the houses of the horoscope is less easy to trace. Aries, Leo and Sagittarius, for instance, are the Fire Signs. With the element fire are associated the ideas of zeal, faith, ardour and inspiration. Planets in the first, fifth and ninth houses unless they be in fiery signs will not indicate these qualities to any marked degree, any more than they will indicate danger through fire, as malefic planets in the fire signs are apt to do.

When Aries, Leo and Sagittarius are tenanted therefore, it may be anticipated that the native's own ardour and faith will be the underlying cause of many of the experiences to which he is attracted and if the progressed aspects are favourable his zealousness will stir up similar reactions among those around him and his inspirations will be a source of benefit to himself and others, often placing him, as a result, at the head of a group. If the aspects are adverse, his own misguided zeal, uncontrolled passions, excessive pride or ill-conceived inspirations may lead him into error.

The fire signs denote what is known as the Bilious temperament. Planets afflicted in these signs warn against intemperate living and are apt to indicate the danger of fevers, inflammatory ailments and troubles which arise from a faulty functioning of the liver. Afflictions involving the Sun, Mars, Jupiter and sometimes Uranus and Pluto in signs of this element threaten danger through fire and the possibility of burns. Excessive heat is apt to prove destructive and for this reason the signs Aries and Leo incline towards barrenness but Sagittarius, on account of its Jupiterian rulership, is moderately fruitful.

Taurus, Virgo and Capricorn are the Earth signs and are related to the realm of practical, everyday routine. They indicate a solid, commonsense and often industrious approach to life on the part of the native and the experiences which he attracts to himself under good aspects involving the earthy signs will bring benefits as a result of his own sound and constructive knowledge of technique, through his adherence to traditional methods and through his ability to keep plodding along at the job in hand. Bad aspects involving these signs are likely to bring setbacks through an over-conservative attitude, a stolid unimaginative approach and a lack of technical and executive ability and practical skill.

The prominence of the Earth element in a birth chart often brings the native into touch with farming or mining, or matters connected with property or estates.

Afflictions involving Taurus, Virgo and Capricorn can sometimes lead to the native being involved in natural calamities such as earthquakes or landslides.

The Earth signs denote what is known as the Nervous temperament and when involved in afflictions often give rise to neurasthenic conditions. In addition the bodily functions and the various processes of the body are often impeded by accretions of ash and other forms of bodily deposits frequently brought about as a result of the native's restricted and unimaginative outlook. Planets in Taurus are generally an indication of fecundity, but Virgo and Capricorn incline towards barrenness.

Gemini, Libra and Aquarius are the Air signs and are related to the intellect. They represent the native's capacity to associate with and to understand the motives of his fellows and indicate a detached and idealistic approach to life. Favourable progressed aspects involving the Air signs show that the native is likely to attract to himself beneficial experiences resulting from his ability to plan and to sow ideas among his fellow men and from his power to mingle with them in a detached way without allowing his emotions to become involved. Adverse aspects warn against losses arising through too much dependence upon theory and too little attention to practical issues or to human values.

Gemini, Libra and Aquarius are apt to denote travel by air when involved with the third or ninth houses or when tenanted by Mercury, Jupiter or Neptune.

The Air signs are not particularly prolific by nature. Gemini inclines towards barrenness while Libra and Aquarius are only moderately fruitful. The Air signs denote what is known as the Sanguine temperament and afflictions in these signs often produce circulatory or mental ailments.

Cancer, Scorpio and Pisces are the Water signs and are related to the native's emotional nature and to his negative, receptive and intuitional side. They indicate an instinctive and highly personalized approach to life. The desire to protect and nourish is strong. Under favourable progressions involving these signs the native will gain through his ability to evoke a sensitive emotional response in others and through discreet and sympathetic behaviour towards them. An intuitive appreciation of their needs and of his own best course of action will help him in making decisions. Adverse progressed aspects involving Water signs are a warning to him to avoid being swayed unduly by his own personal feelings. He may shrink from seizing his opportunities through shyness or some other inhibition. He must not neglect the rational and detached approach to his problems, neither should he rely on his intuition, which will be apt to lead him sadly astray at such times.

When these signs are connected with the third and ninth houses, or with Mercury, Jupiter or Neptune, there is some likelihood of sea voyages. Neptune and Pisces, however, are connected with the idea of boundless space as well as with the watery element, and often indicate travel by air (e.g., Colonel Charles Lindbergh, Mercury in Pisces in the third house, Neptune in Gemini.)

All three of the watery signs are prolific by nature. They denote what is known as the Lymphatic temperament. Afflictions involving these signs are apt to indicate faulty functioning of the glands and may produce watery tumours or ailments, such as dropsy, deriving from the presence of too much moisture in the system. There is some tendency towards anaemia and general lack of tone. In some cases there is a possibility of hypochondria or an addiction to alcohol.

The kind of progressed aspect in force often provides a useful indication of the type of event to be anticipated. When assessing the probable effects of any aspect it is useful to consider that aspect in its relation to the whole zodiacal circle. This may be done in two ways, firstly by dividing the number of degrees contained by the aspect into the 360 degrees of the Zodiac and regarding the number so obtained as having an influence of the nature of a planet, according to the accepted numerical correspondences between planets and numbers; and secondly by measuring off the number of degrees comprising the aspect from the first point of Aries, both clockwise and anti-clockwise in the Zodiac, and anticipating results of the nature of the two signs in which the outer limit of the aspect falls.

By applying these two systems of classification to the conjunction we find that its effects are likely to work out through the sign Aries and in terms of the Sun, for we may regard the conjunction as containing the whole 360 degrees of the Zodiac. The Sun is related to the individuality and the will and driving power of the native, while Aries is initiatory and pioneering in nature. We may therefore expect the conjunction to signal the start of a new phase of experience, in terms of the planet or planets concerned, which will have a direct effect upon the unfoldment of the native's inner potentialities. Its effects are likely to be harmonious or discordant, according to the compatibility of the planets involved.

The semi-sextile is an angle of 30 degrees and is therefore divisible into the Zodiac twelve times. The digits of twelve are reducible, by addition, to three, which is the number of Jupiter. By measuring off 30 degrees in the zodiacal circle in each direction from the first point of Aries we arrive at the beginning of the signs Taurus and Pisces. The semi-sextile is therefore expansive in nature and is related to the building of foundations and the stabilizing of the qualities denoted by the planet or planets and also to the assimilation of those qualities in such a manner that a properly balanced attitude to life as a whole may be maintained. It is likely to have some effect on the financial affairs.

The semi-square aspect of 45 degrees is divisible into the zodiacal circle eight times. Eight is the number of Saturn. Forty-five degrees measured in each direction from the first point of Aries reaches to the middle of the signs Taurus and Aquarius. From these data the semi-square is revealed as having a particular connection with things that are fated to happen, events which the native is unable to avoid and Karma which he is not easily able to modify, for the bonds of Saturn are not easily broken. The sign Taurus shows that the aspect is connected particularly with the way in which the native deals with his resources, while Aquarius places an emphasis on the idealistic side of the nature. Unless these departments in life are well under control the native may lose friends and suffer financially.

The sextile aspect of 60 degrees is a sixth of the zodiacal circle and is of the nature of Venus. The keynote of this aspect is therefore Harmony. It is related to the signs Gemini and Aquarius. Mental activity and idealistic enterprises are much favoured by this aspect which is connected with travel and friendships, and is likely to mark the occurrence of favourable opportunities for advancement.

The square aspect of 90 degrees is one quarter of the zodiacal circle. Four is the number of Uranus. By measuring a quarter of the Zodiac from the first point of Aries we arrive at the beginning of the signs Cancer and Capricorn. The nature of Uranus is erratic and disruptive. The square aspect is apt to signal abrupt changes in the life and produces stresses which rarely appear to be beneficial in their results although they are probably second to none in providing opportunities for soul growth. Effects are most likely to be felt in the domestic sphere and in the professional life. This aspect is a challenge which tests the native's practical approach to life and his reaction to everyday problems. If he is well equipped for the battle of life he is likely to benefit from the controlled use of the force generated by the square but if, on the other hand, he is not able to restrain any wayward impulses he may have, the vibrations of the square are likely to prove extremely disconcerting.

The trine aspect of 120 degrees is divisible into the zodiacal circle three times. Three is the number of Jupiter. The trine measured in the Zodiac from the first point of Aries reaches to the beginning of the signs Leo and Sagittarius. The nature of Jupiter is expansive, that of Leo, creative, and that of Sagittarius speculative and perceptive. These are the qualities of the trine and it is on this account that this aspect is so often the herald of good fortune and success. Emotional pleasure, advancement and travel often result from this aspect, which rarely fails to bring benefits in its train.

The sesquiquadrate aspect, which measures 135 degrees, will not divide into 360 an exact number of times. It is, however, a complementary aspect to the semi-square, since both aspects together form a semi-circle. The semi-square is of the nature of Saturn. If we regard this as a manifestation of the positive qualities of Saturn then it will be permissible to regard the sesquiquadrate as a manifestation of the negative qualities of Saturn. This aspect stretches in the Zodiac to the middle of Leo and the middle of Scorpio. Over-ambition and wrong methods of dealing with resources may cause difficulties and restrictions to arise when this aspect occurs in the progressed horoscope. The failure of enterprises, and financial and health problems are likely.

The quincunx aspect of 150 degrees is another aspect which will not divide exactly into the zodiacal circle. This aspect is the complement of the semi-sextile, for both arcs when united form one half circle. Measured from the first point of Aries the quincunx reaches the corresponding points in Virgo and Scorpio, thus placing an emphasis on matters relating to health, technique, everyday work, service and finance.

There is, however, a deeper meaning to the quincunx aspect which springs from the fact that, considered in terms of the whole zodiacal circle, it is also the complement of the Egyptian Tau aspect of 210 degrees. Measured in the Zodiac in the normal order of the signs, one of the two planets in a quincunx aspect must therefore bear an Eighth House relationship to the other, which in turn is related to the first planet in terms of the Sixth House. The Eighth House has a special connection with regeneration and initiation. The planet which is 150 degrees from the other, measured in the order of the signs, thus derives a Sixth House significance and will therefore denote those faults of character which the native must strive to sublimate, while the other planet will show the means by which he must attempt this task.

From the point of view of the Sixth House the quincunx tests the ability of the native to marshal his resources efficiently and to live in harmony with the laws of nature. This is why the Sixth House is the house of the apprentice and the neophyte, for the Sixth House, and the Eighth House also, is related to our spiritual as well as to our physical health.

The link with the Eighth House is a warning of the critical nature of the aspect, for the path of initiation is always trodden at some peril to the neophyte. For those successful in passing the tests, the rewards are correspondingly great. For those who fail, the hazards and trials are an ordeal which must continually be faced until the aspirant is strong enough to conquer.

The opposition aspect of 180 degrees divides the Zodiac into two hemispheres. Two is the number of the Moon. Libra is the sign which is opposite Aries in the Zodiac. The Moon is a reflector and planets in opposition reflect their qualities into each other. Libra is the sign of harmony. If the qualities denoted by the planets in opposition can be successfully merged the opposition becomes an aspect of culmination, fulfilment and co-operation, and the native will benefit therefrom. If this fusion of qualities is not achieved successfully, friction and discord occur with the result that the opposition becomes an aspect of separation and antagonism. The opposition implies either marriage, in its widest sense, as one extreme or enmity as the other. If there is neither perfect fusion nor complete discord there may be a vacillation between two opposing courses of action or a colourless balanced neutrality.

Chapter V

THE INTERPRETATION OF SECONDARY DIRECTIONS— EXAMPLE READINGS

PART I. PROGRESSIONS INVOLVING THE MIDHEAVEN AND ASCENDANT

THE basic interpretations of planets in aspect to the Midheaven and Ascendant in the progressed horoscope are given below. Each reading is followed by illustrations (taken from the example horoscopes on pages 147–149) which will form a useful basis for study. It should perhaps be stressed that although the cusp of the tenth house is traditionally related to the native's position in the world and the cusp of the first to the physical body and to the native himself, the writer's researches have led him to the belief that it is a mistake to assume that events involving the reputation and worldly standing are wholly related to the Midheaven and that events of a more personal and less public application are wholly related to the Ascendant. Experience does not bear out this contention, for the effects produced by planetary contacts with the Midheaven do not appear to be appreciably different from the effects of the same planetary contacts with the Ascendant. Aspects involving the Ascendant, however, often have a slightly more marked influence on the health of the native, although not invariably so.

The readings which follow cover all possible combinations of progressed and radical positions, for the same type of event is signified whether the aspect is formed between the progressed or converse angle and the radical, progressed or converse planet, or whether it is formed between the progressed or converse planet and the radical angle. It must be remembered that generalisations of this nature cannot be applied haphazardly to every chart. Each nativity must be considered on its own merits and although, generally speaking, a favourable progressed aspect will coincide with events which are beneficial to the native and an unfavourable aspect will signal happenings which affect him adversely, much will depend upon the condition of the various bodies in the nativity. In order to arrive at a detailed judgment, therefore, it is necessary to pay particular attention to the sign and house position of the natal body, as well as to the house ruled by it, together with the aspects which it receives and the aspect, if any, which it forms with the angle in question at birth. Nevertheless, the broad outlines given below should be of considerable assistance to the student in his endeavours to interpret the significance of the progressed horoscope.

SUN—MIDHEAVEN AND SUN—ASCENDANT.
Stimulates creative ability, will to achieve, power of leadership, sense of independence and enterprise (Exs. 1 & 2).

41

Brings opportunities for advancement through merit, ambition, determination or help from superiors (Exs. 3, 4 & 5); consolidating gains; establishing domestic security; purchasing stocks, property and estates; inheriting property; enhancing prestige; gaining spiritual illumination.

May denote marriage (in a woman's horoscope) (Ex. 6); parenthood (Ex. 4).

Brings into contact with those in authority (sometimes patronage of royalty); those in occupations connected with showmanship or display or with those who deal in gold (Ex. 4).

Threatens danger of loss of prestige due to misfortune, false pride, wrong-headedness (Ex. 7) or to the failing fortunes of the father or superiors; domestic setbacks, dwindling estates, damage to property; death of the father (Ex. 8) or a much loved superior, sometimes bringing advancement; (in extreme cases) death of native.

Native is affected by father's affairs (especially in early life); husband's affairs (if a female nativity).

Promotes good health through increased vital powers.

Affects health through depletion of resources through over-exuberance or disappointment over the failure of long-cherished plans; feverish illnesses; ailments affecting back (particularly the dorsal region), heart, spleen, eyes in general (the right eye of a man and the left eye of a woman), blood circulation, vital fluid; sunstroke, fainting fits, bilious attacks; ailments involving parts of the body ruled by the Sun sign and the sign opposite (heat and a large supply of blood is attracted to that part of the body ruled by the Sun sign).

Those destined for permanent fame usually make their mark under solar aspects (Exs. 9 & 10).

EXAMPLES

1. Henry Ford. M.C. r. ♂ ☉. p. Founded Detroit Automobile Company.
2. Henry Ford. Asc. con. △ ☉ con. Founded Ford Motor Company.
3. Cecil Rhodes. Asc. p. △ ☉ con. Prime Minister of Cape Colony.
4. Jay Gould. M.C. con. △ ☉ r. President of Erie Railroad. Birth of daughter. Gold speculations.
5. Jay Gould. Asc. r. ✳ ☉ con. Director of Union Pacific Railroad.
6. Madame Blavatsky. Asc. p. ♂ ☉ con. Marriage. Asc. con. ✳ ☉ r. Second marriage.
7. Cecil Rhodes. M.C. r. ⊼ ☉ con. Resigned Premiership of Cape Colony.
8. Annie Besant. Asc. r. ☍ ☉ p. Father died.
9. Colonel Lindbergh. M.C. p. △ ☉ r. Flew the Atlantic.
10. Adolf Hitler. M.C. p. △ ☉ r. First obsessed with the idea of regenerating Germany.

MOON—MIDHEAVEN AND MOON—ASCENDANT.

(The readings below relate only to aspects formed between the progressed angles and the radical Moon. Aspects to the angles formed by the progressed Moon are too ephemeral to denote anything but comparatively minor effects.

As the lunar orb is greatly affected by the nature of the planets in closest aspect to it and by the sign in which it is placed at birth it is most necessary to pay particular attention to the condition of the radical Moon.)

Stimulates sympathetic nature; domestic, protective and cherishing impulses;

desire for popularity, change and fresh experience; capacity for assimilating experience; reaction to sensation; instinctive reactions acquired as a result of past impressions and sensory experiences.

Brings opportunities for gaining favourable publicity and increased popularity through the widening of contacts; travel or sea voyages (especially if the Moon is in a mutable sign) (Ex. 1).

May denote happenings involving the mother (especially in early life), wife, sisters, daughters, or female relatives and friends (Ex. 2); (in male horoscope) engagement or marriage (Exs. 3 & 4) though rarely without Venusian directions also; changes in career or domestic surroundings (Exs. 5, 6, & 7); motherhood (parturition will be easy or difficult according to the condition of the radical Moon).

Brings into contact with those in the catering and hotel trades; general tradesmen catering for a variety of common needs; nurses, dressmakers or those in occupations connected with water, liquids or silver; people in the mass and particularly the female sex (Ex. 8).

Threatens danger of setbacks to career; diminished popularity; unfavourable domestic changes; ill-health of wife or mother (in extreme cases, bereavement).

Affects health through functional disorders (often encouraged by native's apathy, antipathies, depression or emotional upsets); disturbances of bodily fluids, periodic complaints, dropsy, tumours, indigestion; ailments affecting the stomach, alimentary canal, breasts, uterus, ovaries, lacteals, tear ducts, lymphatics, mucous membranes, brain substance, nerve sheaths, sympathetic nervous system and eyes (particularly the left eye of a man and the right eye of a woman); illnesses affecting parts of the body ruled by the Moon sign and the sign opposite; epilepsy and insanity (if the radical Moon and Mercury are much afflicted).

EXAMPLES

1. Colonel Lindbergh. M.C. con. △ ☽ r. Flew the Atlantic.
2. Karl Marx. M.C. p. ☐ ☽ r. Interfered in daughter's love affair.
3. Prince Bismarck. M.C. con. ☐ ☽ r. Engaged to marry.
4. Ralph Waldo Emerson. Asc. con. ☐ ☽ r. Marriage. (Wife died three years later.)
5. Annie Besant. M.C. p. ☊ ☽ r. Moved house.
6. Mary Baker Eddy. M.C. con. ☊ ☽ r. Repeatedly moved house in order to avoid "malicious animal magnetism".
7. Annie Besant. Asc. con. ☊ ☽ r. Finally made her home in India.
8. Ralph Waldo Emerson. Asc. p. △ ☽ r. Teacher in brother's school for young ladies.

MERCURY—MIDHEAVEN AND MERCURY—ASCENDANT.

(It is most necessary to pay attention to the condition of the radical Mercury as this planet is greatly affected by the nature of the planets in closest aspect to it and by the sign in which it is placed at birth.)

Stimulates powers of adaptability, opportunism, perception and comprehension; ability to grasp and communicate ideas and to establish contacts; activities involving the assimilation of detail and the perception of points of linkage between sundry fields of experience; commercial activities involving fleeting contacts with a variety of people; every means of self-expression at the native's disposal.

Brings opportunities for transmitting ideas through speaking (especially if in public life), writing or publicity (Exs. 1 & 2); increasing knowledge through education (Ex. 3) or travel (Ex. 4), especially in connection with the affairs of the house ruled by Mercury; progress as a result of intelligent forethought or opportunism; gaining scholastic honours.

May denote birth of children (Ex. 5); happenings involving relatives, particularly brothers and sisters (especially in early life) (Ex. 6), neighbours, colleagues and subordinates; changed circumstances in the professional or domestic sphere (Exs. 7 & 8).

Brings into contact with those in occupations connected with transport (Ex. 7), communications, the transmission of ideas and the recording of facts; accountants, bankers, clerks, teachers, journalists, authors (Ex. 4), booksellers, advertisers, interpreters, secretaries, typists, messengers, drivers and conductors of public vehicles, railway and post office employees, adolescents and children of tender years.

Threatens danger of unfortunate changes in the career or upsets in the family circle, especially through the native's own restlessness or lack of intelligent forethought; adverse changes of residence; trouble through slander or malicious gossip; domestic bickering and altercations; mistakes in matters involving detail; (especially when Ascendant is involved) accidents through carelessness or lack of alertness on the part of the native or those around him.

Affects health through restlessness, worry or mental excitement, which has a particular reaction on the respiratory and eliminative systems; headaches, loss of memory, delirium, asthma, hay fever, insomnia, neurasthenia; ailments affecting the Thyroid Gland, hands, upper arms, shoulders, lungs, bronchial tubes, intestines, tongue, vocal chords, the right cerebral hemisphere, the nervous system, nerve fluid, the sense perceptions in general, hearing and seeing in particular, parts of the body ruled by the sign containing Mercury and the sign opposite.

EXAMPLES

1. Karl Marx. M.C. con. △ ☿ p. Editor of radical paper.
2. Jay Gould. Asc. r. ☌ ☿ p. Acquired *New York Times*.
3. Karl Marx. Asc. con. △ ☿ r. Student at the University of Bonn.
4. Ralph Waldo Emerson. Asc. p. ☍ ☿ r. Visited England and met many leading literary figures.
5. Anne Morrow Lindbergh. Asc. p. ✶ ☿ p. Birth of a son.
6. Adolf Hitler. M.C. p. △ ☿ con. Sister Paula born.
7. Jay Gould. M.C. r. △ ☿ p. Became railroad manager. Moved to New York.
8. Mary Baker Eddy. Asc. con. △ ☿ r. Moved house.

VENUS—MIDHEAVEN AND VENUS—ASCENDANT.

Stimulates affections and emotions; desire to achieve harmony in human relationships; artistic susceptibilities.

Brings opportunities for gaining honours, advancement (Ex. 1), popularity— often as a result of native's agreeable and helpful attitude; development of the emotional nature through friendship, romance (Ex. 2), marriage[1] (especially in a male horoscope) (Ex. 3); achievement of success in artistic endeavours; improving financial situation; obtaining comforts and luxuries (this is generally a most pleasant and agreeable period).

May denote the birth of a child (Ex. 4); redecoration or refurnishing of the home; happenings involving the wife, sisters or daughters, or young women in general.

Brings into contact with those connected with music, painting, acting and other artistic pursuits; those engaged in trades which cater for the pleasure of the public or for personal adornment, dress designers, perfumiers, cosmeticians, manufacturers of clothing accessories, florists, hairdressers and confectioners.

Threatens danger of loss of prestige through emotional instability or misplaced affections, through inability or disinclination to blend harmoniously with others or through lazy and lackadaisical behaviour resulting from self-indulgence; loss of material comforts due to straitened circumstances; deterioration of financial resources through an extravagant outlay on luxuries; sorrow through broken attachments often as a result of the native attracting those who cannot live in harmony with him or who will take advantage of his warm-heartedness; accident to or illness of loved ones (in extreme cases—bereavement).

Technically good aspects sometimes coincide with divorce, resignation (Ex. 5), and death (Exs. 6 & 7). Such events may be the only means of restoring harmony when the native is tormented by marital quarrels, duties involving great nervous strain or a severe and prolonged illness.

Promotes good health through a general freedom from worry encouraged by the native's harmonious thinking.

Affects health through over-emotionalism, laxity, erotic tendencies, dietary indiscretions (especially where sweets and sugary confections are concerned) and general over-indulgence; kidney troubles (Ex. 8), tonsillitis, diphtheria, goitre, venereal diseases, lymphatic ailments, throat affections, blood disorders; ailments involving the Thymus Gland, neck, mouth, cheeks, ovaries, oral ducts, general internal reproductive system and the parts of the body ruled by the sign containing Venus and the sign opposite, which are apt to function sluggishly because the bodily ash is deposited there, thus impeding the circulation.

No affliction from Venus need occasion serious alarm unless the planet is badly placed or aspected in the nativity.

EXAMPLES

1. Cecil Rhodes. M.C. r. ✶ ♀ p. Elected Member of Cape Assembly.
2. Prince Bismarck. Asc. p. △ ♀ r. Twice engaged in one year.
3. Colonel Lindbergh. M.C. p. △ ♀ p. Marriage.
4. Mary Baker Eddy. Asc. con. △ ♀ r. Son born.
5. Cecil Rhodes. M.C. con. ☌ ♀ p. Resigned Premiership of Cape Colony.
6. Annie Besant. M.C. con. ☌ ♀ r. Death.
7. Henry Ford. Asc. con. ☌ ♀ r. Death.
8. Mary Baker Eddy. Asc. con. ☍ ♀ con. Renal calculi.

[1] Venus aspects nearly always occur by progression at the time of marriage, not because Venus is the planet of "love" but because marriage is an exercise in maintaining harmony.

MARS—MIDHEAVEN AND MARS—ASCENDANT.

Stimulates energy, drive, initiative; competitive and combative instincts; passional nature as a spur to action and self-assertion.

Brings opportunities for achieving success through energetic and courageous action, often bringing in its train an increase of power (Exs. 1, 2 & 3); clearing away old accumulations as a prelude to future effort.

May denote marriage (in a female nativity, generally at a time when Venus also is active); birth of a son (Exs. 4 & 5)—in later life, a grandson; happenings involving young men; a more than usually active period.

Brings into contact with those in occupations connected with fire, iron and steel; metal workers, engineers, surgeons, dentists, butchers, barbers, policemen, members of the armed forces and those whose pioneering and pugnacious instincts are well to the fore.

Threatens danger of difficulties resulting from foolhardiness, undue haste, or lack of (or wrongly applied) energy and initiative; enmity or domestic strife often arising from the native's own aggressiveness, assertiveness or ill-regulated passions; illness or accident involving a parent or the husband or (in extreme cases) bereavement (Ex. 6) or death of native himself (Exs. 3, 7 & 8); destruction of home or property, especially by fire.

Promotes good health by replenishing stores of energy.

Affects health through depletion of resources as a result of over-exertion, excitability, fits of temper or over-stimulation of passions; sudden, acute and painful diseases, feverish illnesses (Mars generates excessive heat, bringing inflammatory conditions to those parts of the body ruled by the sign containing the planet and the sign opposite); genital disorders, haemorrhage, blood diseases, muscular strains, infections and contagious diseases; ailments affecting the head, nose, bile, motor nerves, motor segment of the spinal cord, left cerebral hemisphere and excretory organs; danger of operations, accidents, cuts, wounds, stabs, bites, stings, burns and scalds, sometimes due to the foolhardiness, carelessness or belligerence of the native or those around him.

EXAMPLES
1. Adolf Hitler. M.C. con. ♂ ♂ p. Fuehrer of Germany.
2. Annie Besant. Asc. p. ✳ ♂ r. President of Indian Home Rule League.
3. Prince Bismarck. M.C. p. ☍ ♂ con. Victory over Austria. Attempted assassination.
4. Jay Gould. Asc. p. ✳ ♂ p. Birth of a son.
5. Karl Marx. M.C. con. △ ♂ r. Birth of a son.
6. Mary Baker Eddy. M.C. r. □ ♂ p. Asc. p. □ ♂ r. Asc. con. ⊼ ♂ r. Death of third husband.
7. Cecil Rhodes. M.C. r. ☍ ♂ con. Death.
8. Madame Blavatsky. Asc. p. ♂ ♂ r. Death.

JUPITER—MIDHEAVEN AND JUPITER—ASCENDANT.

Stimulates powers of growth, increase and expansion on all levels; ability to multiply possessions, social contacts and wisdom.

Brings opportunities for advancement as a result of sound judgment and well regulated actions (Ex. 1) or through the benevolent interest of those in influential positions or the wise counsels of older friends; increasing prosperity, often as a result of the native's own expansive and buoyant attitude (Exs. 2 & 3); gaining popularity and prestige; broadening education through travel, especially in foreign lands (Exs. 4 & 5) or through study (Ex. 6); broadcasting ideas, especially through publishing.

May denote happenings which bring an increase of joyful emotional experience such as engagement (Ex. 7), marriage (Ex. 8), birth of children (Ex. 9) or marriage of children; gain through litigation; involvement in an uncle's affairs; redecoration or refurnishing of the home.

Brings into contact with those connected with big business concerns, philanthropic institutions, the professional classes, especially those connected with the Law, the Church and Universities.

Threatens danger of diminished prestige as a result of faulty judgment, carelessness or the unsound advice of others; financial losses due to extravagance or overoptimism; trouble through legal, religious or educational affairs or publishing; failure of projects either through lack of wisdom or inability to attract support of influential people.

Improves health through sustaining and re-vitalizing the body.

Affects health through illnesses resulting from surfeit and excess or from the native's carelessness and improvidence; over-indulgence, leading to the formation of excess tissue; bodily functions becoming sluggish due to improper working of liver; blood disorders, liver trouble, diabetes, pleurisy, biliousness, gout, heart trouble, high blood pressure, apoplexy; ailments involving the Adrenal Glands, viscera, supra-renals, fibrin in the blood, glycogen in the body, arterial system, right ear, forehead, thighs, hips, feet and those parts of the body ruled by the sign containing Jupiter and the sign opposite. (Jupiterian complaints are best dealt with by fasting, hard exercise and self-denial.)

EXAMPLES

1. Henry Ford. M.C. p. ☌ ♃ r. Asc. p. ✶ ♃ p. Founded Ford Motor Company.
2. Albert Einstein. M.C. con. ☌ ♃ con. First steady job bringing freedom from hardship.
3. Jay Gould. M.C. r. △ ♃ con. Sold Kansas Pacific holdings at huge profit.
4. Albert Einstein. Asc. con. △ ♃ r. Emigrated to Italy. Enjoyed a year's break from school.
5. Anne Morrow Lindbergh. Asc. r. □ ♃ p. Took up residence in England.
6. Karl Marx. M.C. p. ☌ ♃ p. Doctor of Philosophy.
7. Prince Bismarck. Asc. con. ✶ ♃ r. Twice engaged in one year.
8. Prince Bismarck. M.C. con. ☍ ♃ r. Marriage.
9. Jay Gould. Asc. p. ☌ ♃ p. Birth of a son.

SATURN—MIDHEAVEN AND SATURN—ASCENDANT.

Stimulates the native's integrity, stability, perseverance and powers of endurance and self-discipline; ability to organize and concentrate his resources; urge to seek responsibility on all levels and to establish himself thoroughly on a practical basis.

Brings opportunities for advancement as a reward for integrity, dependability and practical commonsense (Ex. 1); slow and steady progress through frugality, perseverance and hard work; realization of ambitions (the native should seek to guard against acting from purely selfish motives); character-building through the shouldering of fresh responsibilities (Ex. 2); stabilizing and consolidating position (Ex. 2); beginning long term projects; serious study, sometimes along religious or philosophical lines.

May denote acquisition of property or land; inheritance of legacies; realization of endowments; changes of fortune due to happenings in the life of the father or an elder relative (particularly in the native's early years).

Brings into contact with older people; those in occupations connected with the land, the building of foundations, or long established institutions; farmers, builders, estate agents, civil servants.

Threatens danger of loss of prestige through lack of self-discipline or a proper sense of responsibility; setbacks as a result of failure to seize opportunities through over-timidity, through shirking obligations or through neglecting to make adequate preparations; separation from or illness of parents or loved ones (Ex. 3) or of business associates sometimes bringing unwanted responsibilities (in extreme cases, bereavement (Exs. 3 & 4) or the death of the native himself (Exs. 5 & 6)); a test of endurance through the discipline of poverty (Ex. 7); inability to attract support as a result of a pessimistic, narrow, self-centred outlook.

Promotes good health through the native's ability to conserve his energies and discipline his body.

Affects health through lowered vitality resulting from the reactions of vague fears and inhibited emotions; ailments arising from malnutrition and lack of self-discipline; accumulations of rheumatic deposits; exposure to cold; imperfect functioning of that part of the body ruled by the sign containing Saturn or the opposite sign (the action of Saturn is to dry up the synovial fluid in the joints of these parts); illnesses of a deep-seated or chronic nature; diseases connected with decay, consumption, gangrene, atrophy; ailments involving the bony structure of the body, the knees and the joints in general, the skin, teeth, hearing apparatus, left ear in particular, gall bladder, pneumo-gastric nerve, sigmoid flexure; rheumatism, spinal ailments, gout, paralysis, deafness, impeded circulation, hardening of the arteries, ankylosed joints; ailments caused by the clogging up of the system or the ageing of the body (Exs. 3 & 8); accidents through falling or crushing.

Under Saturnian directions the necessity for self-discipline is sometimes imposed from without in the form of responsibilities, limitations, delays, frustrations and hampering restrictions.

These directions often work more potently in old age.

The function of Saturn is to stabilize on all levels. That which is to endure must necessarily be free from flaws and weaknesses. Spiritual stabilization is carried out with a strict regard to the debts which the native owes to the past by reason of his previous thoughts and actions. Due reward and just retribution are meted out impartially to the native during the sway of Saturnian directions. If the native falls short in any direction of the perfection which Saturn demands he is apt to suffer for the lack of that quality. If he is well equipped on all levels he will reap the fruits of such preparedness.

EXAMPLES

1. Cecil Rhodes. M.C. con. △ ♄ r. Prime Minister of Cape Colony.
2. Annie Besant. Asc. p. △ ♄ con. Adopted Krishnamurti and his brother. Extensions to Theosophical Society Headquarters at Adyar under her surveillance.
3. Karl Marx. Asc. con. □ ♄ r. Wife died. Ill with pleurisy. Parted from favourite daughter.
4. Adolf Hitler. M.C. p. ♂ ♄ r. Father died.
5. Mary Baker Eddy. M.C. con. □ ♄ r. Death after catching cold.
6. Cecil Rhodes. Asc. con. ☍ ♄ con. Death.
7. Albert Einstein. M.C. p. ♂ ♄ r. & p. Period of unemployment and financial hardship.
8. Madame Blavatsky. Asc. p. ♂ ♄ con. Bright's Disease.

URANUS—MIDHEAVEN AND URANUS—ASCENDANT.

Stimulates the native's powers of originality and ability to act with dynamic individuality without reference to the restraints of convention, tradition and his own inhibitions; will power; independence.

Brings opportunities for advancement and recognition as a reward for originality or independent action (Ex. 1); starting new ventures or making dramatic changes of course (Ex. 2); contacting new ideas (Ex. 3) (sometimes through chance acquaintances) and making new friends; making rapid progress by means of short cuts and labour-saving methods; removing difficulties as a result of a clear-sighted and inspired perception.

May denote the entry into the life of some entirely new factor or the undergoing of a completely new experience; sudden and unexpected happenings (Ex. 4); parenthood; professional or domestic changes (Ex. 2).

Threatens danger of antagonism often aroused by the native's own perverse, abrupt and autocratic behaviour (Exs. 5 & 6) (under adverse aspects he should practise self-discipline and restraint—he should never take the law into his own hands or he will be likely to do more harm than good); sudden upsets (Ex. 7), or break up of domestic conditions, sometimes due to the native's own eccentricities, restlessness or inability to fit in with changed circumstances or conventional patterns; compulsory introduction to new fields of experience; separation or divorce from marriage partner; sudden misfortune to or death of a parent (Ex. 8); in extreme cases, death of the native.

Promotes good health by galvanizing vital forces.

Affects health through excess of vitality, depleted resources or nervous tension; nervous disorders; obscure psychological complexes; cramps, paroxysms, strictures, ruptures, paralysis; ailments involving circulatory system, body electricity, Pituitary Body, parts of the body ruled by the sign containing Uranus and the sign opposite; disorders which develop with unexpected suddenness and are often difficult to diagnose and cure (Ex. 4) (the best results are often obtained through electrical treatment or unorthodox methods of healing); accidents, especially involving electrical apparatus and machines (in rare cases—danger of being struck by lightning).

EXAMPLES

1. Colonel Lindbergh. Asc. p. ☌ ♅ p. Flew the Atlantic.
2. Mary Baker Eddy. M.C. p. ☌ ♅ r. Organized First Church of Christ, Scientist. Founded Christian Science Publishing Society. Moved house.
3. Annie Besant. M.C. p. ⚹ ♅ r. Joined Theosophical Society.
4. Cecil Rhodes. Asc. con. ⊼ ♅ r. Sudden journey to South Africa in search of health. Given six months to live.
5. Adolf Hitler. M.C. con. △ ♅ r. Civil War in Germany.
6. Karl Marx. Asc. con. ☍ ♅ r. Refused entry into Germany after quarrel with Bismarck.
7. Cecil Rhodes. Asc. p. □ ♅ r. & p. Matabele War.
8. Adolf Hitler. M.C. con. □ ♅ r. Father died.

NEPTUNE—MIDHEAVEN AND NEPTUNE—ASCENDANT.

Stimulates altruistic and charitable instincts; artistic sensibilities; idealistic and visionary nature; native's ability to adjust himself to life as a whole and to find his proper level in the world (unless he can maintain complete integrity any benefits forthcoming are likely to be intangible and illusory).

Brings opportunities for fulfilment of some long-cherished desire; gaining widespread popularity through some act which catches popular fancy; residence abroad (Ex. 1) or travels to far horizons (Exs. 2 & 3) especially by air (Neptune is connected with boundless space of any kind); the successful negotiation of problems through a talent for subtle manœuvring derived from a many-sided adaptability.

May denote all kinds of strange experiences calculated to extend the native's horizons—in rare cases the awakening of psychic and other superphysical faculties may bring him into contact with some spiritual or mystical experience which has a profound effect (a select few are able to achieve a mystical realization of the Oneness underlying Existence and so to understand their own part in the Divine Plan) (Ex. 4); the making of sacrifices for some ideal; an inclination to speculate, inflate values (Ex. 5) and indulge in financial jugglery.

Brings into contact with those in careers involving an element of unreality or necessitating contact with far away places; film actors, photographers, artists of all types, airplane pilots, airline employees, those in occupations connected with plastics, oil, drugs, narcotics, chemicals, hospitals, prisons, institutions and animal clinics.

Threatens danger of bitter disappointments and frustrations arising from a fruitless striving to attain perfection or to grasp the intangible (these experiences will be designed to lead the native subtly to the knowledge that the renunciation of worldly appetites and resignation to the Will of God will bring him a serenity of mind which will allow him to pass untroubled through the worst disasters); failure of plans through lack of complete integrity, practical ability, refusal to face up to responsibilities or a distorted viewpoint which gives a false perspective; involvement in muddled or chaotic situations due to a too idealistic, hypersensitive or unreal approach—in extreme cases, some form of obsession (Ex. 6); forced resignation due to pressure of circumstances (Ex. 7); temptations to manipulate odds and to indulge in misleading manœuvres or deception through the duplicity or treachery of others; loss of liberty through sickness or enforced detention; illness of parents or (in extreme cases) bereavement (Ex. 8) or death of native (Ex. 9); suicide (if the afflictions are particularly severe); setbacks to parents.

Affects health through hypersensitivity of body, abnormal expansion, contraction or atrophy of the organs ruled by the sign containing Neptune and the sign opposite; sapping of vital powers resulting from misuse of mental and pyschical energies and the indulgence of depraved appetites; coma, catalepsy, trance, hypochondriac tendencies; diseases of the wasting variety, such as tuberculosis (Ex. 3); ailments involving the Pineal Gland, spinal cord, nerve fibre; rare diseases of obscure origin which are difficult to cure; contact with noxious gases.

During the operation of adverse Neptunian aspects the native should sedulously avoid drugs, alcohol and narcotics and take particular care in the choice of medicines.

EXAMPLES

1. Colonel Lindbergh. Asc. p. ☍ ♆ r. Took up residence in England.
2. Madame Blavatsky. M.C. p. ☐ ♆ r. Travelled to Tibet.
3. Cecil Rhodes. Asc. con. ☐ ♆ r. Contracted tuberculosis. Travelled to South Africa in search of health.
4. Annie Besant. Asc. con. ✶ ♆ r. Founded "Order of the Star", a mystic organization.
5. Jay Gould. Asc. p. ☍ ♆ r. Sold Western Pacific stocks at huge profit.
6. Adolf Hitler. M.C. p. ☐ ♆ r. Obsessed with the idea of regenerating Germany.
7. Cecil Rhodes. M.C.p. ☐ ♆ r. Resigned Premiership of Cape Colony.
8. Prince Bismarck. Asc. con. ☍ ♆ r. Wife died.
9. Ralph Waldo Emerson. M.C. p. ☌ ♆ con. Death.

PLUTO—MIDHEAVEN AND PLUTO—ASCENDANT.

Stimulates the uncovering of resources of all kinds—physical, economic, emoional, mental, spiritual; the native's ability to draw upon the reservoir of the group unconscious and so reinforce the particular qualities denoted by the planets in close aspect to Pluto; desire to achieve regeneration; power of group leadership or ability to join effectively in group action.

Brings opportunities for making new beginnings and entering new phases of experience (Exs. 1 & 2); intensifying experience (Pluto brings about the intensification of a particular type of experience, according to the planet or combination of planets with which it is in aspect. The intensification of any one facet of experience tends to isolate it and throw it into relief. Such an emphasis, if the native is not well balanced within himself, may produce a crisis in his affairs which will cause him to make a complete readjustment of character. Acting on the highest level, Pluto will thus bring about regeneration); gaining advancement and honours (Ex. 3); making progress through an ability to perceive the true motives of those around him and the basic principles underlying his problems; organizing or participating in group action (Ex. 8); improving financial position.

May denote travel (Ex. 3); marriage (Exs. 3 & 4); parenthood (Ex. 4); accidents (especially underground) and violence, if Pluto is afflicted by Mars, Saturn or Uranus; personal suffering as a result of war.

Brings into contact with those who delve or work underground, those who exploit the natural resources of the earth and those who deal with refuse in any form; mineworkers, sewer-men, psychologists (who delve amongst the refuse of the mind), submarine men, uniformed workers, sometimes underworld characters, atomic scientists, those who deal in death and destruction.

Threatens danger of being compelled or conscripted to undertake certain work in order to comply with the needs of a group; coercion by means of gang or mob rule; organized antagonism, sometimes resulting from the native's ruthless behaviour in ignoring the rights of the individual or in making those needs subservient to the needs of a group (Ex. 5); damage to property; financial loss; death of a partner (Exs. 1 & 4) or of a parent (Ex. 6)—in extreme cases, the native's own death (Ex. 7).

Affects health through disorders of the eliminative functions allowing the building up of poisonous deposits in various parts of the system, which act as breeding grounds for diseases, especially those of an epidemic or contagious nature; physical breakdown or those shortcomings attributed to the planet which afflicts Pluto; ailments involving the external sex organs, the nerve centre in the nape of the neck, the spinal fluid, and the parts of the body ruled by the sign containing Pluto and the sign opposite; illnesses resulting from some radical weakness or deep-seated toxic condition (which has long lain dormant) coming suddenly to light, thus producing a crisis; unpleasant and eruptive skin troubles arising from the entry of poisons into the blood stream; injurious hypnotic treatment or the practice of black magic (in rare cases).

EXAMPLES

1. Jay Gould. Asc. p. □ ♀ r. Partner committed suicide. Changed profession.
2. Mary Baker Eddy. Asc. p. ☌ ♀ r. Changed place of residence. Organized First Church of Christ, Scientist. Founded Christian Science Publishing Society.
3. Colonel Lindbergh. M.C. p. △ ♀ r. Marriage, followed by record-breaking flight to the Orient.
4. Mary Baker Eddy. M.C. con. ☍ ♀ r. Marriage. Husband died after six months. Son born.
5. Adolf Hitler. M.C. p. □ ♀ r. One of the ringleaders of the abortive "Bavarian Putsch". Imprisoned.
6. Annie Besant. Asc. p. ☌ ♀ r. Father died.
7. Jay Gould. M.C. con. □ ♀ r. Died.
8. Colonel Lindbergh. Asc. con. ⚹ ♀ r. Joined Air Service of the United States War Department.

Chapter VI

THE INTERPRETATION OF SECONDARY DIRECTIONS—
EXAMPLE READINGS

PART II. SOLAR PROGRESSIONS

WHEN the radical or the progressed Sun is in aspect with a planet by direction, its rays illuminate and vitalize that planet so that all those principles which are represented by the planetary symbol become active and assume prominence in the life. No event of real importance will take place unheralded by an appropriate solar direction. The Sun symbolizes the Life Force and the Higher Self. When it forms progressed aspects with other planets, the faculties and abilities denoted by those planets can be developed and strengthened by a conscious effort of Will, thus reinforcing and confirming the Inner Purpose of the life. If the radical aspect between the Sun and the planet is an adverse one, signifying that the native has difficulties in responding harmoniously to the particular impulses set in motion by the planetary rays, any progressed aspect between the two is apt to re-emphasize the original disharmony. If, however, the progressed aspect is a favourable one, there is a chance that the native will be able to some extent to modify the basic disharmony. When the radical aspect between the Sun and the planet is an harmonious one, there is likely to be less difficulty in overcoming the stresses indicated by an adverse progressed aspect, although the period is hardly likely to pass without imposing some measure of strain on the native.

The following delineations of progressed Solar aspects are given as a guide to interpretation. It must be remembered that a detailed judgment can only be reached after carefully considering the sign and house position of both bodies involved, in addition to the house rulerships of each, the aspect, if any, between the two bodies in the nativity and the aspects which each receives from the other planets in the chart.

SUN—MOON.

Aspects formed while the Sun is moving from the conjunction towards the opposition mark key periods in the active side of the native's life, while corresponding aspects formed while the Sun is moving from the opposition towards the conjunction denote the arrival of important phases in the assimilatory experience of the native. Sextile and trine aspects, and also the semi-sextile, indicate a stimulus to achievement or the reward for past endeavours, according to whether the Sun is moving towards the opposition or the conjunction of the Moon. The semi-square, square and sesquiquadrate aspects show periods of stress when the basic soundness of the native's efforts on all levels will be tested by the impact of events. Any aspect between the two bodies:—

Stimulates a desire for harmonious achievement on all levels.

Brings opportunities for advancement and success following upon a closer integration of the native's desires and feelings with his will to achieve (Ex. 1); expanding consciousness on various levels (the opposition particularly is the aspect of enlightenment—the sextile stimulates mental activity); attracting favour and goodwill by reason of his own increased generosity and benevolence; making new attachments and instituting beneficial changes (Ex. 2).

May denote marriage (Exs. 1 & 3) (the desire for stability linked with the domestic impulses—a blend between the masculine and feminine sides of the nature) but Venus is nearly always active also at such a time; a beneficial period for the native's wife, mother, or sister (Ex. 4).

Threatens danger of lack of success through emotional frustration (inability to co-ordinate inner will to achieve with outer desires and predilections); making ill-advised changes and attracting unfortunate events through inner tension; unpopularity as a result of inability to justify actions to others or to convince them of his true motives; difficult relationships with the opposite sex—not a happy augury for domestic bliss; (in a male horoscope) trouble involving womenfolk, especially the wife and mother—in extreme cases, bereavement (Ex. 5); (in a female horoscope) trouble involving the male sex, especially the husband and the father—in extreme cases, bereavement.

Promotes good health through general freedom from worry.

Affects health through lowered vitality (especially in a woman's chart)—the emotions react strongly on the physical body.

These aspects are very important in a woman's chart. The conjunction often produces a far-reaching crisis, since a great concentration of power is focused upon one point in the Zodiac.

The effects referred to above relate particularly to aspects formed between the progressed Sun and the radical Moon. The progressed Moon also forms aspects with the radical and progressed Sun. These latter aspects are also significant although they are not as far-reaching in their effects, owing to the much faster motion of the Moon. The major aspects, especially the square, conjunction and opposition, seem to have a particular bearing on health matters.

EXAMPLES

1. Albert Einstein. ☉ p. △ ☽ r. Examiner of Patents at Berne, his first steady employment after several years' hardship. Marriage.
2. Jay Gould. ☉ con. ☍ ☽ r. Withdrew from Union Pacific Railroad after realizing a large profit on his shares.
3. Prince Bismarck. ☉ con. ✳ ☽ r. Married.
4. Prince Bismarck. ☉ p. △ ☽ r. Sister married.
5. Ralph Waldo Emerson. ☉ con. ☐ ☽ r. Death of first wife.

SUN—MERCURY.

Stimulates mental activity (Ex. 1).

Brings opportunities for travel; gain through matters connected with transport and communications (Ex. 2); achieving distinction in literary, scholastic (Ex. 3) or newspaper work (in youth sometimes denotes the award of a scholarship); advancement through ability to cope with detail (sometimes appointment to a post of subordinate authority).

May denote changes in the life which make demands upon the native's power of adaptation (Exs. 4 & 5); a prosperous period for brothers and sisters.

Threatens danger of slump in prestige through native paying insufficient attention to detail or through malicious gossip; unwise changes brought about by native's own restlessness; enforced changes caused by circumstances outside his control; setbacks to career due to lack of opportunism or adaptability or to the keenness of rivals who are able to outmanœuvre him.

The adverse aspects seldom denote catastrophic events unless other strong afflictions are also operative.

EXAMPLES

1. Karl Marx. ☉ r. ☌ ☿ con. Began studies at University of Bonn.
2. Jay Gould. ☉ p. ☌ ☿ r. Became a broker in railway stocks.
3. Albert Einstein. ☉ p. ☌ ☿ r. Appointed to special Research Chair at Berlin University.
4. Colonel Lindbergh. ☉ con. ☌ ☿ con. Took up residence in England.
5. Mary Baker Eddy. ☉ con. □ ☿ r. Organized First Church of Christ, Scientist, and Christian Science Publishing Society.

SUN—VENUS.

Stimulates emotions and affections; artistic instincts; harmonious impulses.

Brings opportunities for achieving success in social affairs and in artistic pursuits; gaining advancement (Ex. 1) especially through the support of those in influential positions and through the favour of women; the forming of new attachments; indulging in pleasurable activities.

May denote engagement; marriage (Exs. 2 & 3) (marriage rarely takes place without a Sun-Venus contact, whether or not the partnership is a "love-match", for marriage is an exercise in maintaining harmony, which is the keynote of Venus); birth of a child (Ex. 4); realization of the "heart's desire" (Ex. 5).

Threatens danger of disappointment in matters concerning the affections, either through the native being too eager to please or through not exerting himself sufficiently to maintain harmony in his relationships; losing opportunities for advancement through lack of vigorous action or through laxity in other directions; (in extreme cases) death of loved ones (Ex. 6).

The favourable aspects sometimes coincide with the death of the native (Ex. 7) which often occurs as a happy release after a period of suffering—shown by simultaneous progressed afflictions between other bodies in the horoscope.

The adverse aspects are not usually catastrophic but the native should guard against physical and emotional over-indulgence.

EXAMPLES

1. Cecil Rhodes. ☉ r. ⚹ ♀ p. Prime Minister of Cape Colony.
2. Prince Bismarck. ☉ r. ⚹ ♀ p. Marriage.

3. Ralph Waldo Emerson. ☉ p. ⚹ ♀ r. ☉ p. □ ♀ con. First marriage.
4. Anne Morrow Lindbergh. ☉ r. ⚹ ♀ p. Son born.
5. Madame Blavatsky. ☉ p. ☌ ♀ p. *Secret Doctrine* published.
6. Karl Marx. ☉ r. □ ♀ p. Wife died.
7. Jay Gould. ☉ r. ⚹ ♀ p. Death.

SUN—MARS.

Progressed aspects between the Sun and Mars always mark critical periods in the life. While they are operative the Will is more strongly acted upon by the Desire nature so that, unless the native is completely master of his desires and passions, the " animal " side of his nature is likely to be aroused. He should therefore strive to check his turbulent impulses by the exercise of temperance and discretion and seek to direct his drive and energy into channels beneficial to the community, championing the weak and caring for those less robust than himself.

Any aspect between the two bodies:—

Stimulates energies and passions.

Brings opportunities for advancing interests through energetic action (Ex. 1) and by means of independent and enterprising schemes; undertaking hazardous exploits which demand bold, aggressive measures (sometimes the native joins the armed forces) (Exs. 2, 3 & 4).

May denote marriage (Exs. 3, 4 & 6) (through the stirring up of the passional nature)—especially in a female horoscope; birth of a son (Ex. 5); a long journey (resulting from the urge to action); a strenuous period in which the native is denied luxuries and comforts through force of circumstances.

Threatens danger of setbacks to career through rash and impulsive behaviour and through quarrels and enmity aroused by native's over-assertiveness; losses resulting from extravagance and carelessness; illness or death of loved ones (especially the father)—in extreme cases, the native's own death (Ex. 6); (in a female horoscope) divorce (Ex. 7) or the break-up of the home.

Promotes good health through the increase of vigour and vitality.

Affects health through overheating of the blood; placing extra strain on the heart producing inflammatory or feverish conditions in those parts of the body ruled by the signs containing Sun and Mars and the signs opposite.

EXAMPLES

1. Jay Gould. ☉ r. ⚹ ♂ con. President of Erie Railroad.
2. Colonel Lindbergh. ☉ r. ⊻ ♂ p. Flying Cadet in the Air Service of the U.S. War Department.
3. Colonel Lindbergh. ☉ con. ⚹ ♂ p. Marriage, followed by record-breaking flight to the Orient.
4. Anne Morrow Lindbergh. ☉ p. ☌ ♂ p. Marriage, followed by record-breaking flight to the Orient.
5. Anne Morrow Lindbergh. ☉ con. ⊻ ♂ r. Birth of a son.
6. Adolf Hitler. ☉ p. ☌ ♂ p. Death, preceded by marriage to Eva Braun.
7. Mary Baker Eddy. ☉ p. □ ♂ r. Divorced her husband.

SUN—JUPITER.

Stimulates the urge to expand resources and to increase the range of experience on various levels (Ex. 1); pride in achievement.

Brings opportunities for gaining honour and distinction (Ex. 2); realizing some long cherished ambition (Exs. 3 & 4) often through the benevolent interest of those in influential positions; promotion and financial reward; increased social standing; travel (as a means of gaining wider experience) (Ex. 5).

May denote marriage (Ex. 6) (especially in a female horoscope); birth of a child (Ex. 7).

Threatens danger of damage to prestige through serious errors of judgment often due to over-confidence (in some cases the native may believe that he can break the law with impunity); financial loss through extravagance or self-indulgence; loss of property (Ex. 5); unfavourable ending to lawsuits or religious disputes.

Promotes good health through increased vitality and bodily well-being springing from a general freedom from worry.

Affects health through apoplexy, blood pressure, overworked liver (too much good living clogs the system with rich foods—other bodily functions tend to become sluggish).

The native should live as abstemiously as possible in order to avoid taxing the constitution too heavily.

These contacts always mark important periods in the life and even under adverse aspects some benefits may be anticipated unless both bodies are severely afflicted in the nativity.

EXAMPLES

1. Annie Besant. ☉ p. △ ♃ r. Joined Theosophical Society, of which she eventually became President.
2. Albert Einstein. ☉ p. ✳ ♃ p. Awarded Nobel Prize for Physics.
3. Cecil Rhodes. ☉ con. ☌ ♃ r. First elected to Cape Assembly.
4. Prince Bismarck. ☉ p. △ ♃ r. German Empire proclaimed.
5. Ralph Waldo Emerson. ☉ con. ☍ ♃ con. Travelled to Egypt. House burnt down and rebuilt by popular subscription.
6. Albert Einstein. ☉ con. ☌ ♃ p. Marriage.
7. Annie Besant. ☉ con. ✳ ♃ con. Daughter born.

SUN—SATURN.

Stimulates ambition (Ex. 1) and powers of self-reliance; devotion to duty.

Brings opportunities for promotion to positions of responsibility as a reward for hard work and steady effort (Ex. 2) or through the benevolent interest of older or more experienced colleagues (the native will often find that he will need to draw upon the accumulated wisdom of past experiences in order to discharge his new obligations); increasing moral stature by overcoming selfishness through a discipline of self-abnegation.

May denote a testing period with many stern calls of duty, when the native is called upon to face hardships (Ex. 3) and make sacrifices (the discipline of events will be designed to steady him and to bring home to him his responsibilities and his duty to others and to himself); the start of a new and long term enterprise (Ex. 4)—sometimes marriage (Ex. 5).

Threatens danger of a fall from power (Ex. 6) sometimes due to over-ambition; interference to plans through delays, restrictions and hindrances; inability to seize opportunities as a result of excessive caution or unwarranted doubts and suspicions; loneliness, either through a lack of expansiveness which fails to attract others, through lack of sympathy with those around him or through force of circumstances; setbacks to superiors which may be reflected in the native's less favourable circumstances; trouble involving the father or (in a female nativity) the husband—in extreme circumstances the death of either may bring increased responsibilities (Ex. 7) or, if other testimonies agree, the native himself may die (Ex. 8); checks to career through ill-health; reduced income and losses through property transactions.

Affects health through colds or chills; poor circulation; lowered bodily resistance to disease, often resulting from disappointments and frustrations, which may make the native an easy victim to chronic and deep-seated disorders requiring thorough-going and protracted treatment (Ex. 9).

These aspects test the native's moral fibre to the full in order to determine the extent to which he has succeeded in throwing off the limiting bonds of selfishness and separativeness. He should therefore endeavour to welcome his experiences, however unpleasant they may be, as a means of liberation from the shackles of his karma. By a cheerful acceptance of the decrees of Providence and by diligently cultivating the virtues of hope and courage, he may make more progress on his evolutionary path than he is ever able to realize.

EXAMPLES

1. Adolf Hitler. ○ p. ✶ ♄ r. Proclaimed Fuehrer.
2. Annie Besant. ○ p. □ ♄ r. Elected President of the Theosophical Society.
3. Colonel Lindbergh. ○ con. ☌ ♄ con. Flew the Atlantic.
4. Henry Ford. ○ con. □ ♄ con. Founded Ford Motor Company.
5. Madame Blavatsky. ○ p. ☌ ♄ p. Married Russian diplomat old enough to be her father.
6. Cecil Rhodes. ○ p. □ ♄ con. Resigned Premiership of Cape Colony.
7. Adolf Hitler. ○ p. □ ♄ r. Father died.
8. Cecil Rhodes. ○ con. ☌ ♄ r. (separating). ○ p. □ ♄ p. Death from aneurism of the heart.
9. Cecil Rhodes. ○ p. ✶ ♄ r. Ill with consumption.

SUN—URANUS.

Stimulates dynamic energy and creative talents, sometimes producing spectacular results.

Brings opportunities for inspiring the confidence and enthusiasm of others through personal magnetism and dynamic leadership; gaining new experiences through making unusual contacts, through being in fresh surroundings or through travel (Ex. 1); increasing range of knowledge (Exs. 2 & 3); joining a group or society in order to study some new subject; gain through connection with large corporations.

May denote the successful undertaking of new ventures (Exs. 4 & 5); the beginning of a fresh chapter in the life (Ex. 6); a radical change in the native's philosophy of life or a heightening of inner tension which produces changes in the native's consciousness (one particular event may cause a subtle re-polarization within, bringing about a corresponding alteration of focus in his view of the objective world.)

Threatens danger of sudden and severe setbacks, often due to native's own perverse or wayward behaviour (changes in the bodily magnetism tend to increase any inclinations towards irritability and excitability); arousing enmity by erratic, autocratic behaviour; damage to prestige through rebellious conduct (Ex. 7), general unwillingness to fit in with others or preoccupation with unpractical schemes (the native should seek to harness his dynamic energy in constructive works of vision and originality—he should take particular care to maintain harmony in all his relationships and guard against indulging in erratic behaviour or participating in wild schemes or foolhardy adventures); setbacks to the father or (in a woman's horoscope) the husband, with the possibility of separation or divorce (in extreme cases—bereavement or even death of the native himself); the breaking off of old friendships due to native's fresh interests and altered outlook.

Promotes good health through a fresh influx of dynamic energy.

Affects health through nervous complaints, heart trouble, impaired vitality—often arising as a result of sudden tensions and stresses in the outer life; unusual ailments—the native will often gain most relief through electrical treatment or other unusual curative methods.

EXAMPLES

1. Henry Ford. ☉ p. ⚹ ♅ con. Left home and walked to Detroit to become an apprentice in a machine shop.
2. Albert Einstein. ☉ p. △ ♅ p. General Theory of Relativity published.
3. Madame Blavatsky. ☉ p. ⚻ ♅ r. Successful in entering Tibet, where she received occult teaching.
4. Adolf Hitler. ☉ p. △ ♅ r. & p. Started Second World War which began with the successful invasion of Poland, France, Belgium, Holland and Norway.
5. Albert Einstein. ☉ con. ☍ ♅ r. Examiner of Patents at Berne.
6. Colonel Lindbergh. ☉ p. □ ♅ p. Returned home to United States after four years in Europe.
7. Adolf Hitler. ☉ con. ⚻ ♅ r. Precipitated Civil War in Germany in an attempt to seize power.

SUN—NEPTUNE.

Stimulates emotions and sympathies; philanthropic impulses; yearning for perfection; urge to manœuvre.

Brings opportunities for gaining inspiration and illumination resulting in much spiritual enlightenment (if the native is sufficiently evolved); achieving success through diplomatic skill (Ex. 1) or through a clear-sighted prevision which enables him to anticipate with almost uncanny accuracy the direction which events are likely to take; the realization of some cherished dream (Exs. 2, 3 & 4) though not perhaps in quite the manner expected (there may be some "fly in the ointment" or unforeseen twist); gain through speculation (Ex. 2) or through matters connected with oil, or with sea or air transport.

May denote contacts with the sick and needy which will stimulate a desire to alleviate the sufferings of his fellows (as a result of a heightened appreciation of the common bond between all God's creatures); a refusal to face up to certain circumstances (Ex. 5); the adoption of a pet as an outlet for the affections.

Threatens danger of a peculiarly muddled and involved period in which unwelcome events will produce a strong sense of frustration unless the native has schooled himself to accept willingly the enforced renunciation of something he holds dear (power, position, principles, ties with loved ones (Ex. 6) or even, if other strong afflictions are operative, life itself); financial disaster (an urge for boundless expansion may lead him to become involved in inflationary schemes or unsound gambles—he should endeavour to keep a clear head and a firm sense of perspective and to ensure that any proposed moves are as fool-proof and straightforward as solid, practical commonsense can make them—in extreme cases he may be tempted to take advantage of the weakness of others and seek to make money by means of illegal financial manœuvres: if so, he may forcibly be made to renounce his freedom); loss of prestige through the crafty machinations of envious rivals (Ex. 6) or through irresponsible behaviour (sometimes due to clouding of the judgment by a sense of exaltation)—in extreme cases there may be a danger of illusions or obsessions (Ex. 7); setbacks to career through some unforeseen factor or as a result of some hidden weakness of character becoming manifest (Neptune demands perfection and these aspects often denote events which will test the native's integrity and adjustment to life as a whole—in some cases there is a danger that the native's lower nature and animal instincts will gain the upper hand, so that he is led to commit acts against his better nature and his better judgment); ill health to the father or (in a female nativity) to the husband or to the native himself.

Affects health through sapping of the vitality (hospital treatment or a period of seclusion is often necessary before complete recovery is possible).

EXAMPLES

1. Cecil Rhodes. ☉ con. □ Ψ r. Resident Deputy Commissioner in Bechuanaland where he had to use much diplomacy in handling the natives.
2. Jay Gould. ☉ con. □ Ψ r. Daughter born. Gold speculations.
3. Karl Marx. ☉ con. △ Ψ r. Became engaged and wrote poetry.
4. Karl Marx. ☉ con. □ Ψ r. *Das Kapital* published.
5. Albert Einstein. ☉ p. ⊻ Ψ r. ☉ con. ✶ Ψ r. Ran away from school in Germany to join parents in Italy, feigning sickness in order to do so.
6. Karl Marx. ☉ p. ☍ Ψ p. Wife ill with small-pox. Lost a lawsuit abroad in which he claimed damages for libel.
7. Adolf Hitler. ☉ p. ☌ Ψ r. (applying). Obsessed with idea of regenerating Germany.

SUN—PLUTO.

Stimulates power of self-assertion; desire to demonstrate and gain recognition for abilities.

Brings opportunities for initiating new schemes (Ex. 1) or starting a fresh phase of experience; achievement through dynamic leadership and the ability to weld a group into a solid, cohesive whole and imbue it with singleness of purpose; (at the highest level) achieving Regeneration through Illumination and realization of the true purpose of Life, so bringing about a re-orientation of the life.

May denote an event which isolates the native from his fellows (Ex. 2); a new accentuation of the male principle in the life—in a female nativity, often brings marriage (Ex. 3) (sometimes also in a male chart (Ex. 4)); parenthood; Initiation into new states of consciousness (as at birth and death, or in the case of spiritual rebirth); contacts with those with whom he has a strong karmic bond or events specially connected with the native's destiny (Ex. 2) (the chances of modifying such events are often remote and sometimes there is an element of compulsion or a legal obligation to pursue a certain course).

Threatens danger of setbacks to career or damage to possessions often through forces beyond the native's control (Ex. 5) (he may be unaware of the cause of his undoing until the time for effective action has passed); organized opposition from a group (if either body is badly afflicted in the birth horoscope he may become a victim of mob violence); illness or death of father or (in a female nativity) husband—in extreme cases, death of the native (Ex. 6).

Affects health through the reaction of psychological complexes on the physical system (Ex. 7); long-standing weaknesses suddenly asserting themselves; the stirring up of bodily poisons which have accumulated and lain dormant over a long period; the system becoming more than usually vulnerable to infection; personal injury as a result of war.

This contact is a critical one inasmuch as the native's own thoughts and emotions will be liable to attract to him entities of a like nature, with the result that his desires and feelings will be greatly intensified. It is therefore absolutely essential that he should be constantly on the watch to direct his aspirations only towards the most worthy goals. Failure to use proper discrimination is likely to render him a prey to the dictates of his lower nature. He should therefore concentrate on sending his thoughts outward at this period and should seek to help others as much as possible.

Examples

1. Karl Marx. ☉ con. ☌ ♀ r. *Das Kapital* published.
2. Cecil Rhodes. ☉ p. □ ♀ r. Solitary journey with brother through native territory later to become "Rhodesia".
3. Annie Besant. ☉ con. ☍ ♀ r. (separating). Married after virtually being forced into an engagement.
4. Ralph Waldo Emerson. ☉ con. ⚹ ♀ r. Married. Wife died three years later.
5. Prince Bismarck. ☉ p. □ ♀ r. Resigned position as Minister President of Germany.
6. Adolf Hitler. ☉ con. □ ♀ r. (applying). Death.
7. Prince Bismarck. ☉ con. ⚹ ♀ r. Gravely ill. Finally reconciled with Emperor.

Chapter VII

THE INTERPRETATION OF SECONDARY DIRECTIONS— EXAMPLE READINGS

PART III—LUNAR, INTERPLANETARY AND CUSPAL PROGRESSIONS

THE following delineations of lunar and interplanetary progressions are given as a guide to interpretation. It must be remembered that a detailed judgment can only be reached after carefully considering the sign and house position of both bodies involved, in addition to the house rulerships of each, the aspect, if any, between the two bodies in the nativity and the aspects which each receives from the other planets in the chart.

In the case of progressed aspects involving the Moon only directions involving the radical Moon are included since aspects involving the progressed Moon quickly form and dissolve and, considered by themselves, denote comparatively minor happenings.

MOON—MERCURY.

Stimulates love of activity; desire to exercise adaptability and versatility and to encounter fresh experiences (making the feelings changeable and easily influenced by the mind).

Brings opportunities for making profitable changes; travelling (Ex. 1), speechmaking or literary or scholastic activities (Ex. 2); acquiring a temporary measure of publicity and popularity, often through the making of many casual acquaintances.

May denote activities in connection with transport (Ex. 3) and communications; preoccupation with the affairs of brothers, sisters, young children or neighbours; business changes demanding much attention to detail; domestic changes entailing many minor adjustments (Ex. 4); the announcement of an engagement to marry (Exs. 2 & 5); the making of fresh arrangements for the education of the native's children.

Threatens danger of adverse changes often precipitated by native's own restlessness and lack of stability, and often resulting in unfavourable publicity; difficulties in connection with travel, education (Ex. 6) or publications; (in extreme cases) reversals due to dishonest behaviour (Ex. 7).

Affects health through nervous or mental troubles (other directions should be carefully scrutinized to see whether further warnings of trouble are given.)

EXAMPLES

1. Cecil Rhodes. ☿ con. ☌ ☽ r. First visit to South Africa in order to convalesce.
2. Karl Marx. ☿ con. ☌ ☽ r. Studied at Berlin University. Became engaged.

3. Henry Ford. ☿ p. △ ☽ r. Founded Ford Motor Company.
4. Anne Morrow Lindbergh. ☿ con. ✶ ☽ r. Returned home to the United States after four years in Europe.
5. Annie Besant. ☿ con. ✶ ☽ r. Virtually forced into an engagement.
6. Mary Baker Eddy. ☿ p. ⊼ ☽ r. A year of lawsuits, brought to recover tuition fees from former pupils.
7. Jay Gould. ☿ con. ☍ ☽ r. His fraudulent stock sales were discovered and he was forced to resign from the company and make restitution.

MOON—VENUS.

Stimulates artistic inclinations; harmonious impulses; desires for pleasure and comfort. (Unless other more strenuous directions are operative the native will not feel inclined to assert himself vigorously. He may, in fact, further his interests more effectively by seeking pleasant social contacts.)

Brings opportunities for enjoying much domestic happiness (Ex. 1) and social success; gaining popularity with the female sex (Ex. 2); achieving distinction through artistic endeavour; improving finances; the smooth carrying out of plans.

May denote an emotional attachment (in a male horoscope) (Ex. 3)—sometimes marriage (Ex. 4); parenthood (Ex. 5); pleasant experiences in the life of the mother, sister or other female relative (Ex. 6).

Threatens danger of setbacks through slovenliness or idleness; emotional disappointments often brought about by an over-eagerness to bestow his affections on others; bereavement through the death of wife, mother (Ex. 7) or well-loved friend or female relative (if other strong afflictions are also operative).

Affects health through sluggishness and lack of "tone" in the bodily functions; any desire to clog the system with too many cream pastries and sweetmeats should be strictly discouraged).

EXAMPLES

1. Mary Baker Eddy. ♀ con. △ ☽ r. Husband released from gaol.
2. Ralph Waldo Emerson. ♀ con. △ ☽ r. Taught in brother's school for young ladies.
3. Adolf Hitler. ♀ p. △ ☽ r. First met Eva Braun.
4. Ralph Waldo Emerson. ♀ p. ✶ ☽ r. Second marriage.
5. Jay Gould. ♀ con. △ ☽ r. Son born.
6. Prince Bismarck. ♀ p. ⊼ ☽ r. Sister married.
7. Henry Ford. ♀ con. ⊼ ☽ r. Death of mother.

MOON—MARS.

Stimulates sensations and emotional reactions; desires for change and fresh experience; urges towards vigorous and decisive action.

Brings opportunities for travel (Ex. 1) (the native's restlessness often leads him to embark upon a long journey, often with the avowed intention of searching for adventure); advancement through the use of drive and initiative.

May denote (in male nativity) marriage (Exs. 2 & 3); birth of a child (Exs. 3 & 4).

Threatens danger of domestic discord (Ex. 5); damage to property by fire; setbacks due to his own rash or quarrelsome conduct (he should be careful to exercise as much tact and discretion as possible at this time); illness or trouble involving wife, mother or sister (in extreme cases, bereavement (Exs. 2 & 6) or even native's own death (Ex. 7)); financial losses through extravagant spending.

Affects health through tendency to digestive troubles (especially if the native is apt to let his temper get the better of him); fevers, accidents and burns.

EXAMPLES

1. Colonel Lindbergh. ♂ p. □ ☽ r. Returned home to the United States after four years' residence in Europe.
2. Prince Bismarck. ♂ con. ☌ ☽ r. Death of father. Married while the aspect was still within orbs.
3. Albert Einstein. ♂ p. ✳ ☽ r. Married. A daughter was born while the aspect was still within orbs.
4. Annie Besant. ♂ con. ✳ ☽ r. Daughter born.
5. Mary Baker Eddy. ♂ p. ⊼ ☽ r. Divorced her husband.
6. Adolf Hitler. ♂ con. △ ☽ r. Death of sister.
7. Adolf Hitler. ♂ con. □ ☽ r. Death.

Due to the comparatively slow motion of Jupiter, Saturn, Uranus, Neptune and Pluto, progressed aspects between the radical Moon and these bodies form slowly and remain in force for a number of years. It is likely, therefore, that such aspects will not coincide with clear-cut, well-defined happenings that can immediately be recognised, but they will indicate a period of general success or failure, as the case may be. Nevertheless, as the aspect between the two bodies reaches exactitude it will generally be found that one particular event may readily be identified with the influence of the contact. The events mentioned in the examples all occurred when the aspect was close to exactitude.

MOON—JUPITER.

Stimulates benevolent and expansive impulses; cherishing propensities.

Brings opportunities for gaining prestige and making favourable social contacts as a result of an undercurrent of buoyant optimism which produces favourable reactions from others; expanding knowledge through education (Ex. 1) and travel.

(Events during this period are often highly significant (Exs. 2 & 3) and sometimes productive of great good.)

May denote a particularly smooth running period in the domestic sphere; benefits through the female sex; parenthood (Ex. 4) (a very favourable period for child-bearing); (in a male nativity) marriage (Exs. 5 & 6)—or benefits to the native's womenfolk.

Threatens danger of losses through extravagance or bad judgment; damage to prestige through over-confidence, over-optimism or snobbish behaviour or through the indifference or antipathy of women.

Promotes good health through the smooth working of the bodily functions due to an absence of worry.

Affects health through sluggishness of the bodily functions often brought about by over-eating and self-indulgence (the native should take as much open air exercise as possible at this time).

EXAMPLES

1. Annie Besant. ♃ con. ☌ ☽ r. University Lecturer in Social Science.
2. Adolf Hitler. ♃ con. ☌ ☽ r. Joined the German Workers' Party. He described it as "the most fateful moment of my life".
3. Karl Marx. ♃ con. △ ☽ r. Wrote *Das Kapital.*
4. Jay Gould. ♃ p. □ ☽ r. During this period several offspring were born.
5. Prince Bismarck. ♃ con. □ ☽ r. Married.
6. Karl Marx. ♃ p. △ ☽ r. Married.

MOON—SATURN.

Stimulates powers of concentration and perseverance; cautious tendencies; ense of orderliness.

Brings opportunities for making progress through steady application to the job n hand (often to the exclusion of outside interests) (Ex. 1); stabilizing the feelings nd affections, often through contact with older people, especially older women.

Threatens danger of disappointments, damaged prospects and loneliness often rought about by a fearful, pessimistic, over-cautious approach which frightens way potential helpers or friends (the native should try as far as possible to cultivate buoyant, optimistic outlook); depression due to an undercurrent of restriction and elay or to an uncongenial domestic environment (even under technically "good" spects domestic affairs are apt to pursue a somewhat humdrum course, while under "bad" aspects the native may be forced to submit to an irksome discipline imposed y a dominating mother, or to chafe under the tongue of a nagging wife); sickness r trouble involving wife, mother or sister (in extreme cases, bereavement or death f native (Exs. 2 & 3)).

Affects health through chills; accumulated waste matter in parts of the body ruled y the signs in which the Moon and Saturn are placed and by the signs opposite; shy and rheumatic deposits which impede the workings of the body and restrict he circulation and the free movement of the joints; undernourishment resulting om poverty or hardship; a depressed outlook which lowers the resistance to disease.

Afflictions between the two bodies are particularly unfortunate in a female ativity and sometimes denote difficulty in childbirth.

XAMPLES

1. Karl Marx. ♄ con. ⚹ ☽ r. Founded "Working Men's International". Later, wrote *Das Kapital.*
2. Cecil Rhodes. ♄ con. ∠ ☽ r. Death.
3. Henry Ford. ♄ p. △ ☽ r. Death.

IOON—URANUS.

Stimulates desire for independence and unhampered self-expression; love of hange and novelty; powers of invention.

Brings opportunities for advancement as a result of willingness to experiment with ew and original methods; gaining fresh experience and making new contacts; augurating changes (Ex. 1) (especially domestic changes).

May denote an emotional crisis; publicity or popularity (Ex. 2) (often only temorary); (in a male chart) marriage (Ex. 2); motherhood.

Threatens danger of sudden and unsettling changes (especially in the domestic sphere; notoriety or adverse publicity as a result of erratic behaviour; estrangements or broken attachments (Ex. 3); difficult relationships with women; trouble involving wife, mother or sister (in extreme cases, bereavement).

Affects health through nervous tension (causing indigestion or trouble in those parts of the body ruled by the signs containing the Moon and Uranus or the signs opposite.

EXAMPLES

(In view of the small number of times exact aspects are formed in the example horoscopes, aspects made jointly to both bodies by the progressed angles are also included for purposes of illustration.)

1. Colonel Lindbergh. M.C. p. ⚹ mid-point ☽ ♅ r. Moved to England in search of peace and solitude after the distressing kidnapping and murder of his infant son.
2. Colonel Lindbergh. Asc. p. ☌ mid-point ☽ ♅ r. M.C. con. △ mid-point ☽ ♅ r. Married. Embarked with wife on record-breaking flight to the Orient.
3. Mary Baker Eddy. ♅ con. ∠ ☽ r. Placed her son in charge of the family nurse. This was the prelude to his being adopted and passing out of her life for a number of years.

MOON—NEPTUNE.

Stimulates sense perceptions; aesthetic susceptibilities; sympathies and charitable instincts; imaginative and inspirational tendencies; yearning for perfection; desire for martyrdom.

Brings opportunities for achieving artistic success (if artistic talents are indicated in the nativity) through a heightened emotional response; gaining popularity by some act which catches the popular fancy.

May denote long journeys or voyages (or considerable flights of fancy); domestic changes (Exs. 1 & 2); motherhood; an idealistic attachment; participation in schemes for the welfare of the sick and needy (in some cases the native may have to support his mother, sister or other female relative; involvement in circumstances where there is an element of unreality.

Threatens danger of emotional disappointments (the native may deceive himself by investing his friendships with an unreal glamour, or he may be deceived by others); giving way to a craving for sensation leading to all kinds of unsound experiments and (in extreme cases) to drug taking and other depraved habits; setbacks due to lack of stamina, firmness or a practical commonsense approach to his problems (in some horoscopes this contact may signify escapist tendencies and a complete refusal to face up to the difficulties of life); trouble involving the wife, mother or sister (in extreme cases, bereavement).

Affects health through listlessness, reflected in a general lack of bodily tone.

EXAMPLES

(In view of the small number of times exact aspects are formed in the example horoscopes, aspects made jointly to both bodies by the progressed angles are also included for purposes of illustration.)

1. Anne Morrow Lindbergh. ♆ con. ☌ ☽ r. Returned to the United States after four years in Europe.

2. Colonel Lindbergh. M.C. p. midway between ✱ ☽ r. △ ♆ r. Returned home to United States after four years in Europe.

MOON—PLUTO.

Stimulates domestic instincts; emotional intensity; urge to get to the root of hings; desire to work with or at the head of a group.

Brings opportunities for making radical changes and obtaining completely fresh ontacts and experiences (Ex. 1); gaining popularity through an ability to arouse nass emotions.

May denote a period of many changes or wanderings, bringing varied emotional xperiences, sometimes of an adventurous nature (Ex. 2); (in a male horoscope) narriage; parenthood.

Threatens danger of setbacks as a result of arousing popular antipathy; unfortu-ate changes either due to native's own restlessness or to an element of compulsion; rouble involving the mother, wife or sister (in extreme cases, bereavement (Ex. 3) r death of native (Ex. 4)).

Affects health through extreme sensitivity of the bodily functions, which are easily able to become deranged; digestive troubles.

XAMPLES

(In view of the small number of times exact aspects are formed in the example horo-opes, aspects made jointly to both bodies by the progressed angles are also included for urposes of illustration.)

1. Madame Blavatsky. Asc. p. midway between ✱ ☽ r. △ ♀ r. Succeeded in entering Tibet where she was permitted to acquire much esoteric knowledge.
2. Madame Blavatsky. ♀ con. ☍ ☽ r. With Garibaldi at the Battle of Mentana.
3. Madame Blavatsky. M.C. p. ☍ ☽ r. ☌ ♀ r. Mother died. Went to live with grand-mother.
4. Henry Ford. ♀ con. □ ☽ r. Death.

IERCURY—VENUS.

(These contacts are of comparatively minor importance unless either planet is ıler of the horoscope or is placed close to an angle.)

Stimulates love of peace and harmony; desire for pleasure and comfort.

Brings opportunities for gaining honours and distinctions (Ex. 1); attracting in-reased goodwill through a cheerful attitude of mind and an enhanced ability for lf-expression; achieving success in matters connected with writing, speechmaking Ex. 2) or travelling (Ex. 3); enlisting the help of relatives, neighbours and subor-inates; gain through matters connected with transport (Ex. 4), communications r publicity; enjoying social life (unless other more strenuous progressed aspects re operative, the native will feel no great urge to assert himself); making progress all fields of artistic endeavour.

May denote events which bring peace of mind (Ex. 5); marriage or parenthood Ex. 6); events in the life of a sister (Ex. 7).

Threatens danger of minor upsets as a result of paying too much attention to leasure or arousing the unfavourable comment of women; separation from friends ue to the need to travel.

EXAMPLES

1. Prince Bismarck. ☿ con. ⚹ ♀ r. Minister President of Prussia.
2. Cecil Rhodes. ☿ p. ☌ ♀ p. Elected Member of the Cape Assembly.
3. Madame Blavatsky. ☿ p. ☌ ♀ r. Successful in entering Tibet at second attempt.
4. Jay Gould. ☿ r. ☌ ♀ con. Became a broker in railway stocks.
5. Annie Besant. ☿ p. ⚹ ♀ r. Her children, having come of age, rejoined her after having spent a number of years in the custody of their father.
6. Karl Marx. ☿ p. ☌ ♀ r. Daughters Jenny and Laura born.
7. Adolf Hitler. ☿ p. ☌ ♀ p. Sister Paula born.

MERCURY—MARS.

(These aspects are of considerable importance, owing to the stimulating influence of Mars on Mercury. In order to make the best use of the energies at his disposal it will be necessary for the native to exercise a measure of discrimination and control.)

Stimulates mental processes; spirit of enterprise.

Brings opportunities for advancement as a result of exercising initiative and opportunism; making progress in studies (Exs. 1 & 2); engaging successfully in activities connected with transport (Ex. 3), communications, literature (Exs. 4 & 5), journalism or travel (Ex. 6).

May denote a particularly busy time (but the native should be well equipped to deal with the extra work).

Threatens danger of setbacks due to ill-formed judgments resulting from hasty, impulsive reactions and over-excitability (even under good aspects the urge to rash and precipitate action is not easily curbed by those of immature moral stature so that much energy may be wasted upon feverish activity that accomplishes little); arousing antagonism through sarcastic speech and an assertive manner (in extreme cases the native may become involved in libel or slander actions—he should use great discrimination and restraint if he sets anything on paper); quarrels with relatives, neighbours or subordinates; reverses in matters connected with transport (Ex. 7), communications or journalism; anxiety occasioned by the illness of a child or relative (in extreme cases, bereavement); a temptation to gain ends by fraudulent means (if the nativity suggests a lack of integrity).

Affects health through nervous strain due to over-work (if Mercury and the Moon are greatly afflicted at birth there may be mental disorders); lung troubles; ailments involving the hands, arms or intestines.

EXAMPLES

1. Karl Marx. ☿ p. ⚹ ♂ p. Student at the University of Bonn.
2. Karl Marx. ☿ r. ⚹ ♂ p. Awarded Degree as Doctor of Philosophy.
3. Henry Ford. ☿ r. ☌ ♂ con. Founded Ford Motor Company.
4. Mary Baker Eddy. ☿ con. ☌ ♂ r. Wrote first draft of her book on Christian Science.
5. Ralph Waldo Emerson. ☿ p. ⚹ ♂ p. Visited Great Britain, meeting many of the leading literary figures of the day.
6. Albert Einstein. ☿ p. □ ♂ r. Emigrated to Italy, running away from school to do so.
7. Colonel Lindbergh. ☿ p. ☌ ♂ r. Resigned from the United States Army Air Corps.

MERCURY—JUPITER.

Stimulates expansion of ideas; buoyancy of outlook.

Brings opportunities for gaining fresh experience and expanding knowledge through travel (Exs. 1 & 2); achieving success in connection with writing (Ex. 6), publicity, communications, transport (Ex. 3), publishing, education (Ex. 4) or as a result of the helpful co-operation of relatives, neighbours and subordinates; advancement as a result of sound judgment and a more mature and optimistic outlook than usual, which attracts the increased interest of those in authority; enjoying a smooth-running period during which he will be able to order the small details of everyday routine to suit his convenience.

May denote parenthood (Exs. 5 & 6); success in litigation.

Threatens danger of setbacks and losses due to mistakes of judgment brought about by over-optimism and carelessness; depletion of finances through extravagance; lack of success in litigation.

Affects health through lung trouble (Ex. 7).

EXAMPLES

1. Madame Blavatsky. ☿ con. ☍ ♃ r. First travels abroad.
2. Colonel Lindbergh. ☿ con. ☌ ♃ con. Record-breaking flight across the Atlantic.
3. Henry Ford. ☿ con. △ ♃ con. Founded Detroit Motor Company.
4. Albert Einstein. ☿ p. ✶ ♃ r. Occupied the Chair of Physics at the University of Prague, improving his prestige and financial standing.
5. Mary Baker Eddy. ☿ con. ☌ ♃ r. Adopted one of her followers as a son.
6. Annie Besant. ☿ p. △ ♃ r. Son born. First short stories published.
7. Karl Marx. ☿ p. ☍ ♃ p. Died of lung trouble.

MERCURY—SATURN.

Stimulates mental concentration; preoccupation with the more serious side of life (Ex. 1).

Brings opportunities for achieving success in connection with writing, education, transport (Exs. 2 & 3) or communications or as result of prudent forethought and careful attention to detail; increasing knowledge through deep and prolonged study (sometimes through the practice of meditation).

May denote the undertaking of some arduous and possibly lonely task, calling for much mental stamina (Exs. 4, 5, 6 & 7).

Threatens danger of disappointments and frustrations sometimes due to native's pessimistic or self-centred attitude repulsing those who might have offered their co-operation (he should seek to cultivate a more positive and buoyant approach to his problems, putting aside all fear of failure, remembering that obstacles exist to be overcome and that worry and anxiety are barriers to his ultimate success that only he can remove); delays to plans on account of the imperfection of some small detail; difficulties in connection with travel, study or literary activities; trouble with relatives, neighbours or subordinates; anxiety occasioned by the serious illness of a child or near relative (in extreme cases, bereavement) (Ex. 8).

Affects health through lowering of the bodily resistance as a result of disappointments causing a depressed state of mind (this may lead to mental trouble if the Moon and Mercury are much afflicted in the nativity); sluggish reaction of the nervous system; rheumatic trouble affecting the limbs; slow mental reactions causing loss of mobility (Ex. 9).

Examples

1. Ralph Waldo Emerson. ☿ con. △ ♄ r. Became a student at Cambridge Divinity School.
2. Henry Ford. ☿ p. ☌ ♄ p. Founded Detroit Motor Company.
3. Jay Gould. ☿ con. ☍ ♄ r. Became President of the Erie Railroad.
4. Colonel Lindbergh. ☿ con. ☌ ♄ r. Embarked on record-breaking flight to the Orient
5. Karl Marx. ☿ con. ☌ ♄ con. Wrote *Das Kapital.*
6. Henry Ford. ☿ con. □ ♄ r. Left home, walked to Detroit, apprenticed himself in a machine shop and worked for a jeweller in the evenings to pay for his board He was working fourteen hours a day.
7. Cecil Rhodes. ☿ p. □ ♄ r. Went with his brother on a solitary journey through the territory later known as Rhodesia.
8. Annie Besant. ☿ con. ⊼ ♄ r. Death of younger brother.
9. Annie Besant. ☿ con. ⊼ ♄ con. Became ill after a fall.

MERCURY—URANUS.

Stimulates desire to broaden mental perspective; inventiveness; determination and assertiveness.

Brings opportunities for exercising originality and contacting new ideas (Ex. 1 or seeing already known facts in a new light, often in a flash of inspiration; achieving success in study or matters connected with publications, transport (Ex. 2) or com munications; gaining fresh experiences through travel (Exs. 3 & 4).

May denote parenthood (Exs. 1, 2 & 3); unexpected news of relatives or neigh bours; sudden changes precipitated by the native's own restlessness;

(In some cases marriage occurs while this contact is operative (Exs. 1 & 3) This appears to be due to the fact that the native finds himself faced with a completely new set of circumstances as a result of living in partnership.)

Threatens danger of setbacks (Ex. 5) often due to stubborn adherence to wrong ideas or to the native's restless desire for novelty unsettling those around him and so paving the way for an unsympathetic reception of his projects (he should try to medi tate quietly and regularly upon his problems, reflecting upon the virtues of prudence and discretion); arousing opposition through open rebellion against a system which he regards as oppressive; reverses in connection with matters relating to study travel, communications or literary work (Ex. 6).

Affects health through nervous tension or nervous spasms (if Mercury and the Moon are much afflicted in the nativity there may be some danger of mental trouble) lung trouble.

Examples

1. Albert Einstein. ☿ p. △ ♅ r. Examiner of Patents at Berne. (This aspect lasted for several years owing to the slow motion of Mercury. While it was operative he married and his wife gave birth to a son. This period has been described as his most mentally productive phase, "the harvest years of genius".)

2. Jay Gould. ☿ p. △ ♅ r. Elected President of the Erie Railroad. Daughter born.
3. Colonel Lindbergh. ☿ p. ⚹ ♅ r. Record-breaking Atlantic flight.
(Owing to Mercury turning direct during this period the aspect remained within orbs for several years, during which time he married, embarked on a record-breaking flight to the Orient, and became the father of a baby son.)
4. Madame Blavatsky. ☿ p. △ ♅ r. With Garibaldi at the Battle of Mentana.
5. Cecil Rhodes. ☿ con. ☌ ♅ con. Resigned Premiership of Cape Colony.
6. Karl Marx. ☿ con. □ ♅ r. Services terminated after ten years as foreign correspondent of a New York newspaper. This marked the end of his journalistic work.

MERCURY—NEPTUNE.

Stimulates mental sensitivity; powers of imagination; aesthetic sensibilities.

Brings opportunities for gaining inspiration through an intuitive perception (by seeking to still the mind and so increasing its receptivity, the native will be able to derive the maximum advantage from this contact); achieving success in creative work as a result of a sensitive awareness; making long-distance travels by sea or air (Exs. 1, 2 & 3); engaging in profitable enterprises in connection with transport (Ex. 4), communications, literary work or education (Ex. 5).

May denote contact with ideas which open up fresh horizons (Exs. 6 & 7); involvement in peculiarly chaotic conditions often brought about by the native's relaxed and sometimes nebulous frame of mind.

Threatens danger of setbacks due to a lack of drive and purpose (a listless yearning after the unattainable and a tendency to vague and muddled thinking must be replaced by a vigorous plan of action aimed at some immediate and worth-while goal within reach); losses resulting from unprofitable investigations or from grave errors of judgment due to an element of self-deception; an unusual illness affecting a child or near relative (in extreme cases, bereavement); being deceived by relatives, neighbours or subordinates.

Affects health through hypersensitivity of the nervous system; a tendency to suffer from delusions (in extreme cases)—(sanity may be threatened if Mercury and the Moon are both heavily afflicted in the nativity); a general listlessness reflected in a lack of bodily "tone".

Examples

1. Colonel Lindbergh. ☿ con. ⊼ ♆ r. Became a Flying Cadet in the Air Service of the War Department.
2. Anne Morrow Lindbergh. ☿ con. ⚹ ♆ con. Returned to the United States after four years in Europe.
3. Annie Besant. ☿ p. □ ♆ p. Visited Australasia as President of the Theosophical Society.
4. Henry Ford. ☿ p. ☍ ♆ p. Founded Detroit Motor Company.
5. Annie Besant. ☿ p. □ ♆ r. Joined the staff of the *National Reformer*. Spent the period touring and lecturing.
6. Madame Blavatsky. ☿ con. ☍ ♆ r. Successfully entered Tibet where she was allowed to gather much occult knowledge.
7. Karl Marx. ☿ con. △ ♆ r. This contact was operative in his late twenties, a period which was described as "vital in the development of his ideas".

MERCURY—PLUTO.

Stimulates a desire to study those things which lie beneath the surface; all Mercurial activities (Ex. 1).

Brings opportunities for making progress in all forms of study and research (Ex. 2); travelling (Ex. 3), speechmaking (Ex. 4), or undertaking literary work or activities in connection with transport or communications; gaining the helpful co-operation of relatives, neighbours or subordinates.

May denote parenthood.

Threatens danger of setbacks due to the native falling a prey to wrong ideas brought about by some form of mass suggestion or arising from some inner compulsion (in some cases these ideas may become a dominating obsession, to be carried out at all costs (Ex. 5)—in extreme cases, if Mercury and the Moon are severely afflicted in the nativity, his mental balance may be permanently disturbed); bereavement through the death of a son or daughter (Exs. 6 & 7), near relative (Ex. 8), neighbour or subordinate (in extreme cases, death of the native himself) (Exs. 7 & 9).

Affects health through hypersensitivity of the nervous system increasing the liability of the system to infection and derangement; lung trouble (Ex. 8).

Examples

1. Karl Marx. ☿ p. ⚹ ♇ r. This aspect was within orbs for several years during his late twenties. These were vital years in the development of his ideas. While the contact was operative he became editor of a radical paper and was expelled from Prussia for writing seditious articles.
2. Madame Blavatsky. ☿ con. ⚹ ♇ r. Formally admitted to the Buddhist religion.
3. Madame Blavatsky. ☿ p. ☍ ♇ r. Returned to Russia after ten years of extensive travel in foreign lands.
4. Cecil Rhodes. ☿ p. △ ♇ r. Elected a Member of the Cape Assembly.
5. Adolf Hitler. ☿ con. □ ♇ r. First became obsessed with the idea of regenerating Germany.
6. Colonel Lindbergh. ☿ con. ⚻ ♇ r. Child kidnapped and murdered.
7. Henry Ford. ☿ p. ⚻ ♇ r. Mercury was stationary over a period of several years. During this period his son died and then his own death occurred.
8. Annie Besant. ☿ p. ⚻ ♇ r. Suffered with congestion of the lungs. Mother died.
9. Cecil Rhodes. ☿ con. ☌ ♇ r. Death.

VENUS—MARS.

Stimulates affections; social instincts; passionate impulses; desire to achieve harmony in human relationships.

Brings opportunities for making pleasant social contacts with the opposite sex; indulging in pleasurable activities; making peace with adversaries.

May denote a love affair (Ex. 1) (especially while the native is young); marriage (Exs. 2, 3 & 4) (this contact is often an important factor) or a more ardent relationship with the marriage partner; parenthood (Ex. 5); events in the life of brothers, sisters, sons or daughters (Exs. 6, 7 & 8).

Threatens danger of disappointments in love resulting from over-ardent or too passionate behaviour or from the intervention of a rival (the native should strive to practise control over his desires and not let his heart rule his head or he may suffer some grievous setbacks); damage to prestige through scandal involving the opposite sex; accident to or illness of loved ones (in extreme cases, bereavement) (Exs. 5, 6 & 9).

EXAMPLES

1. Prince Bismarck. ♀ con. ✶ ♂ r. Engaged for the third time. The engagement was broken.
2. Henry Ford. ♀ con. ☌ ♂ r. Married.
3. Albert Einstein. ♀ p. □ ♂ p. First marriage, which was later dissolved.
4. Albert Einstein. ♀ con. ✶ ♂ con. Second marriage.
5. Colonel Lindbergh. ♀ con. ☌ ♂ r. Baby son kidnapped and murdered. Second child born.
6. Mary Baker Eddy. ♀ p. □ ♂ r. Brother married. Death of mother.
7. Karl Marx. ♀ con. □ ♂ con. Daughter Laura married and made her home in France.
8. Annie Besant. ♀ con. ⚻ ♂ r. Lost the custody of her daughter as the result of a lawsuit brought by her husband.
9. Albert Einstein. ♀ p. ⚻ ♂ r. Death of second wife.

VENUS—JUPITER.

Stimulates expansion of emotions and affections; harmonious social impulses; love of ease and comfort.

Brings opportunities for gaining honours and advancement (Exs. 1 & 2); improving financial position; achieving success in professional work (this is often a period of smooth and easy expansion (Ex. 3) sometimes due to the native's increased sociability which helps to attract the support of women and those in influential positions).

May denote marriage (Ex. 4); parenthood (Ex. 5); a successful period in the life of the native's sister, wife or daughter (Ex. 6).

Threatens danger of frittering away good opportunites through giving way to a lethargic and easygoing mood which encourages slovenly work (unless other more strenuous directions are also operative); emotional disappointments as a result of bestowing the affections indiscriminately.

(As both planets are benefics an adverse aspect seldom heralds a major catastrophe.)

Affects health through increased self-indulgence (there is often a desire to augment the intake of rich foods and so put on weight—much will depend upon the native's age and normal health as to whether the consequent clogging of the system is likely to involve any serious threat to the bodily well-being—it will be a good plan for him to take regular daily exercise and to practise living as abstemiously as possible while this contact is operative.)

EXAMPLES

1. Adolf Hitler. ♀ p. △ ♃ p. Became Fuehrer of Germany.
2. Cecil Rhodes. ♀ con. ☍ ♃ con. Appointed Deputy Resident Commissioner in Bechuanaland. By his sympathetic understanding of the natives he did much to gain their goodwill.
3. Adolf Hitler. ♀ p. △ ♃ r. Outbreak of Second World War. (In spite of the fact that

hostilities took place, Germany made rapid territorial gains at a very low cost in men and materials.)

4. Ralph Waldo Emerson. ♀ p. △ ♃ p. Married.
5. Jay Gould. ♀ r. ☌ ♃ p. Son born.
6. Mary Baker Eddy. ♀ p. △ ♃ r. Sister married.

VENUS—SATURN.

Stimulates control of the emotions.

Brings opportunities for advancement as a result of steady and sober effort (the native will often be brought into contact with those older than himself so that he may gain by their wisdom and experience); improving the financial position through long-term investments.

May denote a stabilizing of the emotions through friendship with those whose affections are steadfast and reliable (often the native is brought into contact with women of maturer years); marriage (Ex. 1) (bonds of affection formed under this contact are likely to endure); a prosperous period for the father (especially in early life).

Threatens danger of emotional disappointments (Exs. 2 & 3), sometimes due to the native's inability to arouse a sufficient response from the object of his affections; quarrels or estrangements resulting from a lack of sympathy with the emotional problems of others (Ex. 4); an illness to the wife, mother or daughter (in extreme cases, bereavement (Exs. 5, 6 & 7) or native's own death (Ex. 8)).

Affects health through a depressed state of mind resulting from emotional frustration and causing a lowering of resistance to disease (Ex. 6) which often encourages a relaxed throat or sluggish functioning of the kidneys.

Examples

1. Prince Bismarck. ♀ p. △ ♄ p. Married.
2. Annie Besant. ♀ con. ☍ ♄ con. (applying). Thrown over in favour of Gandhi by the Indian Home Rule League after two years' devoted work as their President.
3. Karl Marx. ♀ p. ⚻ ♄ r. Parted from his daughter Tussy in order to travel for the sake of his health.
4. Prince Bismarck. ♀ con. ☌ ♄ r. & p. (applying). Interfered in son's love affair, which was broken off as a result.
5. Henry Ford. ♀ p. ☌ ♄ p. Death of mother.
6. Karl Marx. ♀ con. ☌ ♄ con. Death of wife. Ill with pleurisy.
7. Prince Bismarck. ♀ p. ☍ ♄ r. Death of wife.
8. Prince Bismarck. ♀ p. ☍ ♄ p. Death.
9. Cecil Rhodes. ♀ con. ☌ ♄ r. ♀ p. △ ♄ r. Death from aneurism of the heart.

VENUS—URANUS.

Stimulates emotional tension; artistic talent.

Brings opportunities for gaining honours and distinctions (Ex. 1) sometimes as a result of the exercise of ingenuity; developing aesthetic susceptibilities; gaining artistic inspiration through a sudden raising of the consciousness following a period of emotional tension; improving the financial position from unexpected sources or through sudden transactions; securing the goodwill of the female sex; forming interesting new friendships and making fresh social contacts; establishing independence.

May denote unexpected and sudden developments in the emotional life (Ex. 2) (the native is likely to encounter people and situations calculated to quicken his emotions); a romantic attachment (especially in a male nativity) (Exs. 3 & 4)—such attachments may be quickly entered upon and as quickly broken unless other directions hold the promise of a more permanent arrangement; the temporary prominence of one particular woman in the native's life; a most beneficial period for his wife or daughter; parenthood (Ex. 5).

Threatens danger of unfortunate love affairs owing to the native being too impressionable; tension in relationships leading to estrangements, broken attachments or even divorce (Exs. 6 & 7) often as a result of difficulty in controlling impulsive surges of emotion (by paying too much regard to the dictates of his feelings he will be tempted to act in an erratic manner with too little thought for the feelings of others); setbacks due to motives being misconstrued and actions misinterpreted (Ex. 8); interference with native's comfort or settled conditions (Ex. 7); illness of wife or daughter (Ex. 8) (in extreme cases, bereavement (Exs. 9 & 10)).

Affects health through throat or kidney ailments (Ex. 11).

EXAMPLES

1. Cecil Rhodes. ♀ p. △ ♅ p. Prime Minister of Cape Colony.
2. Prince Bismarck. ♀ p. △ ♅ r. Reconciled with the Emperor after his resignation from the Chancellorship.
3. Prince Bismarck. ♀ con. △ ♅ con. Twice engaged in the space of a year. Both engagements were broken.
4. Karl Marx. ♀ p. ☍ ♅ con. Became engaged. Wrote poetry.
5. Karl Marx. ♀ con. △ ♅ r. Son Guido born.
6. Mary Baker Eddy. ♀ p. □ ♅ p. Husband sent to prison.
7. Mary Baker Eddy. ♀ p. □ ♅ r. Second husband deserted her. She was evicted from her lodgings in straitened circumstances.
8. Karl Marx. ♀ p. ⊼ ♅ r. Wife had small-pox. He lost a lawsuit for libel, brought in the Prussian courts.
9. Madame Blavatsky. ♀ p. △ ♅ r. Taken into grandmother's charge after her mother's death.
10. Adolf Hitler. ♀ con. ⊼ ♅ p. Owing to the slow motion of Venus this aspect was in operation for several years. During this period both his father and his mother died.
11. Madame Blavatsky. ♀ con. ☍ ♅ r. Ill with Bright's disease.

VENUS—NEPTUNE.

Stimulates emotional sensitivity; idealistic aspirations (Ex. 1); aesthetic susceptibilities; charitable instincts; desire for peace and harmony (Ex. 2).

Brings opportunities for raising the whole emotional level so that the period is hardly likely to pass without the native experiencing some inner joy (if his religious impulses are well developed it may be possible for him to gain illumination by means of visions or through arriving at a state of ecstasy); gaining increased popularity (Ex. 3) especially with women; enjoying pleasant emotional experiences (Ex. 4)—

sometimes a romantic attachment of an idealistic character or resulting from some strange fascination; artistic inspiration (and, if either planet is strongly placed in the nativity, much creative fecundity); improving financial position through matters connected with the sea, with oil, or with some large scale enterprise (Ex. 5).

May denote the birth of a daughter (Ex. 4).

Threatens danger of emotional difficulties due to a temporary parting from the beloved or through the termination of a love affair; attracting scandalous comment as a result of a clandestine attachment or an unworthy infatuation; suffering bitter disappointments through chasing illusory pleasures (unless the native can learn to renounce all desire for personal gratification through the emotions he is likely to nurse many sorrows); financial losses, sometimes due to a temptation to make "easy money" (he should beware of short cuts to fame and fortune as unforeseen snags and unlooked for disappointments may tantalize him as he seeks to grasp his prize); setbacks due to lack of drive (the native may indulge in an orgy of self-pity over some emotional disappointment which will cause him to neglect favourable opportunities for advancement—even under favourable directions there is likely to be some degree of self-indulgence which will work out to his disadvantage); trouble or illness involving a loved one (in extreme cases, bereavement (Ex. 6) or death of the native (Ex. 7)).

Affects health through a lowering of the bodily tone resulting from disappointments and disillusionments, rendering the system more than usually liable to infection; lack of self-discipline in habits; relaxed throat, sluggish functioning of the kidneys or contamination of the venous blood stream.

EXAMPLES

1. Ralph Waldo Emerson. ♀ p. ☍ ♆ r. Attended Cambridge Divinity School.
2. Annie Besant. ♀ p. △ ♆ p. Launched campaign for Indian freedom.
3. Colonel Lindbergh. ♀ con. △ ♆ r. Made record-breaking flight across the Atlantic. While the aspect was still within orbs he married and made a record-breaking flight to the Orient.
4. Karl Marx. ♀ con. △ ♆ r. First met Engels, one of his few real friends. Daughter Jenny born.
5. Jay Gould. ♀ con. △ ♆ r. Withdrew from Union Pacific Railroad Company after selling his shares at a huge profit.
6. Albert Einstein. ♀ con. ☐ ♆ r. Wife died.
7. Jay Gould. ♀ p. ☍ ♆ r. Died of tuberculosis.

VENUS—PLUTO.

Stimulates emotional activity; artistic sensibilities.

Brings opportunities for achieving success (Ex. 1), gaining popularity, forming new friendships and making helpful contacts, often as the result of a cheerful and adaptable frame of mind; developing any latent ability to undertake creative artistic work as a result of enhanced emotional susceptibilities (in some cases the native may join a group specializing in artistic activity).

May denote a romantic attachment (in any case a young woman with whom the native has a karmic link is apt to play an important part in the life at this time) marriage (Exs. 2, 3 & 4); birth of a daughter or a granddaughter (sometimes a son, if both planets are in masculine signs); events in the life of a daughter (Ex. 5).

Threatens danger of setbacks to prestige sometimes resulting from an inability to work in harmony with others (schemes depending for their success upon the goodwill of a group or large organization are not likely to flourish at this time); emotional disappointments, bringing keen suffering; an unfortunate love affair; illness or accident involving a loved one (in extreme cases, bereavement or the native's own death (Ex. 6)).

Affects health through lowered resistance following upon emotional distress (Ex. 7) and disappointments involving the affections; disorders of the throat and kidneys; blood poisoning (Ex. 8); (the native should avoid clogging the system through over-indulgence in sweet, sugary and sickly foods).

EXAMPLES

1. Cecil Rhodes. ♀ p. △ ♀ r. Elected a member of Cape Assembly.
2. Prince Bismarck. ♀ con. ☌ ♀ r. Married.
3. Karl Marx. ♀ con. ⌄ ♀ r. Married.
4. Mary Baker Eddy. ♀ p. ☍ ♀ r. Second marriage.
5. Karl Marx. ♀ con. ☌ ♀ r. Daughter Laura married and made her home in France.
6. Prince Bismarck. ♀ con. ✶ ♀ r. Died.
7. Cecil Rhodes. ♀ con. ✶ ♀ r. Having been given six months to live he journeyed to South Africa to regain his health, which he did.
8. Karl Marx. ♀ p. △ ♀ r. Suffered from an attack of carbuncles.

MARS—JUPITER.

Stimulates enthusiasm, desire for energetic and enterprising self-expression (Ex. 1) (on the physical, emotional, mental or spiritual level (Ex. 2), according to the type of horoscope and the native's evolutionary status—much will depend upon whether he can temper his enthusiasm with wise judgment or whether he allows it to run away with him and lead him into rash and ill-considered behaviour).

Brings opportunities for gaining advancement through drive and initiative or in recognition of achievements (Ex. 3); enlisting the support of others and imbuing them with some of his confidence; increasing income and expanding resources (often coinciding with an increased outlay as a means of attracting further business); multiplying social contacts; expanding experience through long journeys or frequent travel.

May denote marriage (especially in a female nativity) (Exs. 1 & 4); birth of a son (Exs. 4, 5 & 6); beneficial periods in the son's life.

Threatens danger of setbacks due to a reckless lack of restraint, to uncontrolled zeal or to an impulsive, unbridled egotism (Ex. 7) (adverse aspects are often a severe test of the native's accumulated wisdom and the extent to which he can control the promptings of his animal passions through the exercise of prudence and discretion—he must strive to mobilize his resources wisely and to discipline his impetuosity—such precautions are doubly necessary when either planet is much afflicted in the nativity or when the radical Saturn is not strong); financial losses due to extravagance, over-optimism and ill-advised speculations (this is not a time to lend or borrow money!); involvement in religious quarrels sometimes following upon a surge of religious feeling; difficulties while travelling (Ex. 8); adverse legal decisions; in extreme cases, bereavement (Exs. 4 & 9).

EXAMPLES

1. Anne Morrow Lindbergh. ♂ con. ☌ ♃ r. Married and embarked with husband on a record-breaking flight to the Orient.
2. Ralph Waldo Emerson. ♂ con. ✶ ♃ con. Attended Cambridge Divinity School.
3. Albert Einstein. ♂ p. ☌ ♃ r. Elected a Member of the Royal Society. Awarded the Nobel Prize for Physics.
4. Mary Baker Eddy. ♂ con. ☌ ♃ r. Married. Husband died after six months. Three months later a son was born.
5. Annie Besant. ♂ r. ✶ ♃ con. Son born.
6. Jay Gould. ♂ p. ✶ ♃ p. Son born.
7. Adolf Hitler. ♂ con. □ ♃ r. (applying). Second World War began.
8. Madame Blavatsky. ♂ con. ☍ ♃ con. Unsuccessfully attempted to gain entry into Tibet.
9. Henry Ford. ♂ p. ☌ ♃ r. Death of son.

MARS—SATURN.

Stimulates courage and determination; ambition; staying power.

Brings opportunities for the realization of ambitions as a result of vigorous and determined efforts and constructively applied exertions (Ex. 1); making steady progress as a result of concentrating on essentials and dispensing with elaborate plans (Ex. 2); clearing the ground for fresh undertakings by means of hard spadework.

May denote a period when the native will be required to live hardily and to undertake much dirty, laborious or even dangerous work; a test of the native's will power, when he will be required to control and direct the fiery energy of Mars by means of the stern discipline of Saturn (during the struggle there is a danger that his sympathies may be pushed into the background and he must take care not to become too intolerant of others as he steadily pushes his own interests—in order to counteract such a tendency he should seek to champion those weaker than himself and to exert himself strenuously for some righteous cause).

Threatens danger of attracting quarrels, disputes and unpleasant experiences often as a result of giving way to passions and acting in a turbulent manner (Ex. 3) (especially if Mars is the more prominent)—in extreme cases the native may take the law into his own hands and resort to violence (Ex. 4) or he may have violence done to him; losing good opportunities for advancement through lack of initiative or through too much concern for his own safety (if Saturn overpowers Mars); losses through damage to property (Ex. 5); strained relationships with superiors (sometimes the sympathies of the father or an older relative may be alienated); misfortune involving the native's father or son (in extreme cases, bereavement or death of the native (Exs. 6 & 7)).

Affects health through the reaction of considerable inner stress and tension on the physical body (Ex. 8); depletion of energies following a period of physical or mental strain (Ex. 9); accidents, especially as the result of a fall, often involving broken bones, wounds or bruises (no major calamity need be feared unless the Ascendant is also subject to violent progressed afflictions).

Examples

1. Adolf Hitler. ♂ con. △ ♄ con. Became Fuehrer of Germany.
2. Annie Besant. ♂ con. ✱ ♄ r. Elected President of the Blavatsky Lodge shortly after joining the Theosophical Society.
3. Mary Baker Eddy. ♂ p. □ ♄ r. Rebellion among her students, who objected to her dictatorial methods.
4. Adolf Hitler. ♂ con. △ ♄ r. Ordered the ruthless "Blood Purge" of the Nazi Party.
5. Ralph Waldo Emerson. ♂ p. ☌ ♄ p. House burnt down but rebuilt by popular subscription.
6. Prince Bismarck. ♂ r. ☌ ♄ con. Death.
7. Adolf Hitler. ♂ r. □ ♄ p. Death.
8. Cecil Rhodes. ♂ con. ☌ ♄ r. Health broke down. Travelled to South Africa and worked on brother's farm in Natal.
9. Karl Marx. ♂ p. ⊼ ♄ p. Suffered from an attack of carbuncles.

MARS—URANUS.

Stimulates forceful and assertive tendencies; creative and pioneering instincts.

Brings opportunities for achieving success, often in a relatively short time, through sudden spurts of purposeful activity and through unexpected manœuvres (Ex. 1); removing opposition by the force of personal magnetism; gaining advancement as a result of opportunism, resilience, resourcefulness and drive (Ex. 2); obtaining benefit through machinery or as a result of mechanical ability (Ex. 3) (the native may learn to drive a car while this contact is operative); demonstrating originality in a practical manner (Ex. 4).

May denote the breaking up of old conditions as a prelude to entering upon a new cycle of experience (sudden, unexpected events will often cause the native to alter some of his preconceived ideas and turn his attention to fresh fields of endeavour); novel experiences through travel (Ex. 5), often undertaken at short notice and arising through unforeseen circumstances; marriage (in female horoscope) (Ex. 6).

Threatens danger of setbacks, often due to the native's irritable and excitable nature; loss of prestige resulting from wrongly applied initiative (enterprises of too novel a nature are not likely to flourish at this time); arousing enmity through lack of tact, autocratic behaviour or through some subtle inner tension which attracts those inimical to his interests while repelling potential allies (Exs. 1 & 7); awkward situations involving the opposite sex (in female nativity); trouble involving a son; in extreme cases, bereavement (Exs. 8, 9, 10 & 11) or death of the native (Exs. 11 & 12).

Affects health through nervous tension (Exs. 8 & 10) (the native should relax as much as possible); muscular strain; proneness to accidents (more than usual care is needed during this period for the contact may denote accidents through fire, explosions, electrical apparatus or machinery, although a major catastrophe is not likely to occur unless the Ascendant is also involved in strong progressed afflictions).

(Owing to the forceful nature of the two planets the period during which the contact is formed is often a critical one).

EXAMPLES

1. Prince Bismarck. ♂ p. □ ♅ r. Victory over Austria. Attempt on life.
2. Cecil Rhodes. ♂ con. ☌ ♅ r. Prime Minister of Cape Colony.
3. Henry Ford. ♂ p. □ ♅ r. Founded Ford Motor Company.
4. Albert Einstein. ♂ con. △ ♅ con. Elected to a special Chair of Research at Berlin University.
5. Madame Blavatsky. ♂ con. ☍ ♅ r. With Garibaldi at the Battle of Mentana.
6. Mary Baker Eddy. ♂ con. △ ♅ con. Married for the third time.
7. Cecil Rhodes. ♂ con. ☌ ♅ con. Matabele War.
8. Prince Bismarck. ♂ con. ☌ ♅ r. Gravely ill. Brother died.
9. Colonel Lindbergh. ♂ p. □ ♅ r. Baby kidnapped and murdered.
10. Karl Marx. ♂ con. ☍ ♅ r. Death of wife. Ill with pleurisy.
11. Karl Marx. ♂ con. ☍ ♅ r. Death of daughter Jenny. He died from lung trouble two months later.
12. Cecil Rhodes. ♂ p. ⚹ ♅ r. Death.

MARS—NEPTUNE.

Stimulates the desire nature in a subtle fashion; idealism as an inspiration to action.

Brings opportunities for gaining advancement by tackling problems in a spirit of idealistic enthusiasm which communicates itself to those around; making progress by means of indirect action and by a diplomatic and strategic approach; undertaking long distance travel (Exs. 1 & 2) and activities in connection with propaganda (Exs. 1 & 3).

May denote retirement from active work (Ex. 4); some act of self-denial or devotion performed under the spur of a deep religious impulse; unaccountable attractions and repulsions; a sudden and uncontrollable urge towards some course of action which quickly expends itself, leaving the native high and dry after the first wave of enthusiasm has subsided; marriage (Exs. 2 & 5) (in this connection the contact relates particularly to the stirring up of the emotional side of the nature); a desire to speculate (Ex. 6).

Threatens danger of being carried away by impulsive surges of emotion and so acting unwisely (the native should carefully analyse his motives and seek to behave with scrupulous honesty at this time or he may become involved in dealings of a highly questionable nature); coming into contact with unsavoury environments or falling in with undesirable companions who will exert a bad influence over him (it is vitally necessary for the native to curb his appetites and passions and to cultivate purity of thought during the operation of these aspects—in extreme cases, he may find himself engulfed in a whirlpool of sense gratification which will drag him down to the lowest depths of depravity); victimization through arousing secret enmity and becoming the subject of slanderous accusations; trouble involving a son; being imposed upon by the opposite sex (in female nativity); bereavement (Exs. 4 & 7) or death of the native (Ex. 8) (in extreme cases).

Affects health through the contamination of the blood stream (the native should be on his guard against impure or polluted foods—defective drains may sometimes be a source of trouble); a tendency to disperse the physical energies fruitlessly or to allow the physical resources to be sapped through worry or foolish habits, so opening the door for hostile organisms to invade the system (in some cases the native may suffer from some form of wasting illness which is difficult to cure on account of the prevailing psychic conditions); accidents involving steam or noxious gases (no major catastrophe need be feared unless the Ascendant is also involved in strong progressed afflictions).

EXAMPLES

1. Annie Besant. ♂ con. ✶ Ψ r. Embarked on a lecture tour of Australasia.
2. Madame Blavatsky. ♂ con. ⊼ Ψ r. Married an elderly diplomat a month before her seventeenth birthday. Separation followed almost immediately and she set out on extensive foreign travels.
3. Karl Marx. ♂ con. ☍ Ψ r. Wrote *Das Kapital*.
4. Ralph Waldo Emerson. ♂ con. △ Ψ r. Wife died. Deeply depressed in health and spirits, he retired from his office as pastor.
5. Ralph Waldo Emerson. ♂ p. ☐ Ψ r. Married.
6. Jay Gould. ♂ con. ✶ Ψ r. Gold speculations.
7. Henry Ford. ♂ p. ⊼ Ψ r. & p. Mother died.
8. Henry Ford. ♂ con. ☐ Ψ r. & con. Died.

MARS—PLUTO.

Stimulates self-assertiveness; desires and passions.

Brings opportunities for gaining objectives by vigorous, determined (and sometimes violent) action (Exs. 1 & 4); exercising powers of leadership and initiative (through his courageous bearing and confident attitude the native will be able to imbue those around him with an enthusiasm and a fighting spirit similar to his own) (Exs. 2 & 3); clearing the ground as a preliminary to constructive action.

May denote a spell of hard physical exercise (the native may be able to call forth reserves of strength the existence of which he had hardly suspected); marriage (Exs. 2 & 4); the birth of a son; contact with death in some form (Exs. 5 & 6); considerable preoccupation with the affairs ruled by the house which bears the sign Scorpio on the cusp (since both planets have dignity in this sign).

Threatens danger of setbacks resulting from rash, precipitate or unrestrained action (during this period the native is likely to respond more quickly to all forms of excitement and much will depend on the extent to which he has succeeded in sublimating his animal nature); arousing antagonism through acting too forcefully and without due regard for the rights and feelings of others (in extreme cases there may be a temptation to take the law into his own hands with a reckless disregard for any consideration but the dictates of his own anger, jealousy or fanaticism); unpleasant attentions from members of the opposite sex (in a female nativity); bereavement (Ex. 7) or death of the native himself (Exs. 7 & 8) (he may become the victim of violence at the hands of some gang, sometimes as the result of a feud—no major catastrophe need be feared unless other strong progressed afflictions are also operative at this time).

Promotes good health through the mobilization of the bodily energies.

Affects health through feverish illnesses; impurity of the blood stream (Exs. 9 & 10); accidents (these aspects often denote physical pain); an operation on that part of the body ruled by the sign in which either planet is placed or by the sign opposite.

EXAMPLES

1. Prince Bismarck. ♂ con. □ ♀ r. Franco-German War.
2. Anne Morrow Lindbergh. ♂ p. ⋎ ♀ r. Married and embarked with her husband on a record-breaking flight to the Orient.
3. Colonel Lindbergh. ♂ p. □ ♀ r. Made record-breaking flight across the Atlantic.
4. Henry Ford. ♂ con. □ ♀ r. Married. Built his own house.
5. Jay Gould. ♂ con. ☌ ♀ r. ♂ p. ⋎ ♀ r. Business partner committed suicide.
6. Albert Einstein. ♂ p. □ ♀ r. Friend Adler sentenced to death for having assassinated the Prime Minister of Austria. He was later reprieved.
7. Karl Marx. ♂ p. ⊼ ♀ r. While this aspect was operative he was ill with pleurisy, his wife and daughter Tussy died and he himself finally succumbed as a result of lung trouble.
8. Cecil Rhodes. ♂ con. ☌ ♀ r. Death.
9. Karl Marx. ♂ con. □ ♀ p. Suffered from an attack of carbuncles.
10. Karl Marx. ♂ con. □ ♀ r. Second attack of carbuncles.

ASPECTS BETWEEN THE MAJOR PLANETS

Owing to the slow motion of the major planets, progressed aspects between them will remain operative over a long period, consequently their influence is more likely to colour the general background of the whole period rather than to indicate a continuous series of specific events. Nevertheless it should be remembered that in the great majority of cases where an exact aspect is formed by progression between two major planets, those planets will have been within orbs of that aspect at birth. Aspects such as these occurring in the nativity denote inherent capacities and qualities in the native which he will be able to express and make manifest to the greatest extent when an exact contact is made between the two planets by progression. It is for this reason that the progressed aspects, although forming slowly, assume a major importance in the chart during the period in which they approach and reach exactitude. At this time it will generally be found that at least one significant event will take place which can clearly be traced to the intrinsic nature of the two planets involved.

This period will mark the crux of the native's development in so far as that particular planetary blend is concerned and will bring opportunities allowing him to extract the maximum benefit from his experiences.

If, while the two major planets are still within a degree of an exact aspect with each other, one of the progressed angles of the chart, or a faster moving planet, also forms an aspect with one of these planets, this will act as a powerful stimulus and produce further significant events of the nature of the planets involved.

In the examples given all the events occurred when the aspects were exact or close to exactitude.

JUPITER—SATURN.

Stimulates development of wisdom; powers of judgment; ability to organize resources.

Brings opportunities for gaining advancement as a result of integrity and hard work; undertaking increased responsibilities as a means of developing judgment and expanding wisdom; (Exs. 1 & 2); gradually building up and expanding resources (favours the acquisition of wealth and property) through the exercise of sound business sense.

May denote gain through matters connected with the Law and with religion (Exs. 3 & 4); a legacy; a prosperous time for the father (especially when the native is young).

Threatens danger of missed opportunities, either through lack of initiative or foresight or through a desire to avoid responsibility; setbacks due to extravagant habits and an over-optimistic frame of mind (if Jupiter is the stronger) or to a parsimonious streak and a fearful, pessimistic outlook (if Saturn gains the upper hand)—should both planets be fairly evenly balanced the native may vacillate between extremes of expansiveness and cautious timidity with the result that his efforts are ill-timed and lacking in stability; unstable financial position in early life due to the failing fortunes of the father—later, a possibility of straitened circumstances (Ex. 5) or losses due to unwise speculation, unsound investments or deterioration of property and depletion of resources through having to contribute to the parent's upkeep (the native should not lend money or take financial risks during this period); adverse decisions in lawsuits; disputes over religious matters (Ex. 6); bereavement (Ex. 7) or death of the native himself (in extreme cases) (Exs. 8 & 9).

Promotes good health through the sound working of the liver and a freedom from deposits of "ash" which clog the system.

Affects health through sluggish functioning of the liver (careful attention to diet and the avoidance of too many rich foods will do much to counteract this tendency); arterio-sclerosis (in later life).

EXAMPLES
  1. Albert Einstein. ♃ p. ⚹ ♄ r. Appointed to the Chair of Physics at Prague University, and later to the special Chair of Research at the University of Berlin.
  2. Prince Bismarck. ♃ con. △ ♄ r. Took over the additional duties of Minister for Commerce.
  3. Mary Baker Eddy. ♃ p. ☌ ♄ r. Received much unfavourable publicity in the closing years of her life as a result of a lawsuit brought to prove that she was no longer capable of managing her affairs. She won the suit.
  4. Annie Besant. ♃ con. △ ♄ r. Founded the Order of the Star, a group pledged to prepare for the coming of a new World Teacher.
  5. Mary Baker Eddy. ♃ con. ☌ ♄ con. In straitened circumstances after being deserted by her second husband.
  6. Mary Baker Eddy. ♃ con. ☌ ♄ r. Argued about predestination with the Elders of the Congregational Church when being examined for admittance.
  7. Anne Morrow Lindbergh. ♃ con. □ ♄ con. Death of father. Baby son kidnapped and murdered.
  8. Cecil Rhodes. ♃ con. ⚻ ♄ con. Died from an aneurism of the heart.
  9. Jay Gould. ♃ p. □ ♄ r. (applying). Death.

JUPITER—URANUS.

Stimulates originality; desire for independence; religious instincts (Ex. 1); urge to explore the realms of knowledge or to travel at large in the physical world (Ex. 2); intuitive judgment through flashes of inspiration.

Brings opportunities for gaining advancement through the adroit handling of affairs (if the native is able to respond in full measure to these vibrations he will be able to develop a dynamic enthusiasm which will communicate itself to others and thus enable him to play a leading part in the organization of a group dedicated to the furtherance of his ideas); achieving success in matters connected with the Law, publishing, travel (Exs. 4 & 5) religion and places of learning (Ex. 3); making considerable progress in the study of occult and out-of-the-ordinary subjects; improving the financial position, especially through dealings connected with inventions (Ex. 6), with large corporations or with undertakings connected with electricity.

May denote some rather unexpected or sudden chain of events which is likely to work out to the native's advantage (Ex. 7); marriage (Exs. 6, 7 & 8).

Threatens danger of setbacks due to wrong-headedness (the native may gain a position of power only to misuse his authority) and mistakes of judgment (often as a result of giving way to short-lived enthusiasms which lead him into unprofitable commitments); losses through faulty speculation, unsuccessful litigation, matters connected with publishing or through a temptation to make an extravagant outlay on personal ostentation; strange and unexpected mishaps while travelling which may prove expensive and troublesome; becoming involved in religious disputes.

Affects health through inefficient and erratic functioning of the liver (the native would be well advised to avoid any eccentricities of diet calculated to put too much strain on the liver). (The contact is often a factor in cases of diabetes.)

Since the function of Uranus is to break up the limiting bonds of Saturn and since the effect of Jupiter is to expand the influence of those planets with which it is in contact, it will be clear that an adverse aspect between the two bodies must be disastrous to one who lacks the balance and restraint of a good Saturn. It will behove the native to cultivate a cautious and commonsense approach to his problems while an adverse aspect between Jupiter and Uranus is operative, or he may involve himself in many troubles through a lack of basic stability, constancy or moral purpose.

EXAMPLES

1. Mary Baker Eddy. ♃ p. △ ♅ p. Argued with the Elders of the Congregational Church on a point concerning predestination when being examined for admittance into the Church.
2. Madame Blavatsky. ♃ p. ☌ ♅ con. With Garibaldi at the Battle of Mentana.
3. Prince Bismarck. ♃ con. ✶ ♅ r. Studied Law at Gotenberg University.
4. Colonel Lindbergh. ♃ con. ⊻ ♅ r. Returned to the United States after four years' stay in England.
5. Albert Einstein. ♃ p. ☍ ♅ r. Ran away from school in Germany to join parents who had emigrated to Italy.
6. Albert Einstein. ♃ p. ☍ ♅ con. Examiner of Patents at Berne. He married while the aspect was still operative.
7. Henry Ford. ♃ p. △ ♅ r. Offered forty acres by his father in an attempt to draw him away from his interest in mechanics. While the aspect was still operating he married and built his own house.
8. Mary Baker Eddy. ♃ p. △ ♅ r. First marriage.

JUPITER—NEPTUNE.

Stimulates finer susceptibilities; religious instincts; generous impulses.

Brings opportunities for refining judgment by means of a sensitive intuition; acquiring popularity and prestige through charitable enterprises and philanthropic gestures; attracting good fortune as a result of a kindly and expansive attitude; improving the financial position especially through investing in large scale enterprises or in concerns connected with oil or air and sea transport (under this contact the native is often able to develop an uncanny flair for financial matters so that he is able to gain handsomely through speculation); making progress in matters connected with religion, law, publishing (Ex. 1), travel and higher education (Exs. 2 & 3).

May denote marriage (Ex. 4)—on account of the accompanying expansion of the emotions; the practice of renunciation or self-denial in some form, giving the native an emotional sense of self-exaltation; a strong accent on those affairs connected with the house bearing the sign Pisces on the cusp (since both planets have dignity in that sign).

Threatens danger of difficulties resulting from over-impulsiveness or setbacks due to the cultivation of an unreal sense of values or an inflated opinion of his capabilities (the increased susceptibilities and enlarged emotional response resulting from this contact may throw the native off his balance, even under technically "favourable" aspects, unless he is able to practise the Saturnian virtues of stability, thrift and practical commonsense—if Neptune is the stronger he may live in a world of fantasy and so be unfitted to deal with some of the sterner aspects of life); reverses in connection with litigation or matters related to religion, publishing or travel; losses due to sickness, carelessness or an irresponsible tendency to rely on "hunches" and unsound information (in some cases chaotic financial manipulations may lead him into deep waters or he may be defrauded by unscrupulous associates); financial reverses in matters connected with sea or air transport, oil or gases; bereavement or the death of the native himself (in extreme cases) (Ex. 5).

Affects health through nervous debility or eyestrain. (Sometimes there is a danger of accidents with gas or noxious fumes.)

EXAMPLES

1. Madame Blavatsky. ♃ con. ⚹ ♆ r. *The Secret Doctrine* published.
2. Albert Einstein. ♃ p. ⚹ ♆ con. Awarded the Gold Medal of the Royal Astronomical Society for his work in connection with the Theory of Relativity.
3. Albert Einstein. ♃ p. ⚹ ♆ r. Appointed Professor of Mathematics at Princeton University.
4. Mary Baker Eddy. ♃ p. △ ♆ r. First marriage.
5. Henry Ford. ♃ p. ⊼ ♆ r. Death.

JUPITER—PLUTO.

Stimulates enthusiasm; exuberance; positive, expansive tendencies; desire for independence; penetrative abilities.

Brings opportunities for achieving success through a self-assurance which attracts the confidence and support of influential patrons; gaining in popularity as a result of a jovial participation in social activities, leading to useful business contacts; engaging in group activities; making progress in matters connected with religion, law, publishing, travel (Exs. 1 & 2) and higher education; improving financial position through activities or investments connected with the mineral resources of the earth.

May denote gains through legacies.

Threatens danger of losses through waste and extravagance (the native should restrain any strong urge to gamble or speculate); setbacks due to an inability to discipline his impulsiveness (in extreme cases there may be a desire to take the law into his own hands or a difficulty in restraining his appetites and desires) (Ex. 3); adverse decisions in litigation; disputes over religious matters, sometimes arising out of the native's fanatical or bigoted views; illness or death of relatives or friends (Ex. 4), which may involve him in considerable expense.

Promotes good health through increased vitality.

Affects health through the rash expenditure of the physical resources and the scattering of energies, so that the resistance to disease is lowered—the liver is likely to be the most vulnerable organ.

EXAMPLES

1. Anne Morrow Lindbergh. ♃ r. ☌ ♀ con. While this aspect was operative she spent four years in Europe.
2. Albert Einstein. ♃ con. □ ♀ r. Joined his parents, who had emigrated to Italy. He ran away from school in Germany to do so, his education being interrupted for a year.
3. Adolf Hitler. ♃ con. ⊼ ♀ r. Instigated the Blood Purge of the Nazi Party.
4. Jay Gould. Asc. p. ☌ ♃ r. □ ♀ r. Business partner committed suicide.

(The last illustration is included owing to the shortage of progressed Jupiter-Pluto contacts in the example horoscopes.)

SATURN—URANUS.

Stimulates powers of organization; constructive abilities; desire to transcend physical limitations.

Brings opportunities for gaining advancement or improving financial position through an ability to concentrate resources and blend a strong will with a dynamic imagination (Exs. 1, 2 & 3); overcoming obstacles by means of a determined and energetic approach, thus paving the way for sound and practical constructive work; enlisting the aid of experienced associates who will provide the native with fresh ideas and thus stimulate his inventive abilities; perfecting the Uranian faculties of clairvoyance and clairaudience (if the native is sufficiently advanced).

May denote a period of considerable stress during which the impact of events will be designed to break up crystallizations of habit and outlook as a preliminary to the awakening of the consciousness to those things which lie outside and beyond the self (as it is difficult to achieve an easy blend between the rays of Saturn and Uranus—unless the aspect between them is a favourable one and both planets are fairly well aspected in the nativity—the native is apt to suffer through this break up of settled conditions, which will be likely to produce a feeling of instability and insecurity that will react to his disadvantage); changes (in early life) due to altered circumstances in the father's life; changes occurring through the intervention of older people; prominence of those affairs ruled by the house bearing the sign Aquarius on the cusp (since both planets have dignity in that sign) (Ex. 4).

Threatens danger of setbacks through a failure to grasp opportunities or a lack of sufficient originality or clarity of vision (if Saturn is the stronger), through a stubborn adherence to misguided ideas (Ex. 5) or a tendency to be too domineering which may alienate the sympathies of potential helpers (if Uranus is the stronger)—in rare cases the native may penalize himself by being unselfish to a point beyond all reason or he may stoically resign himself to what he believes to be an immutable fate; reduced circumstances in early life due to father's reverses; illness or accident involving an older relative (in extreme cases bereavement (Ex. 6) or death of the native himself); violence to the native (no major disaster need be feared unless there are simultaneous progressed afflictions involving the angles of the horoscope).

Promotes good health through well regulated nervous reactions.

Affects health through stresses and strains which undermine the native's resistance to disease (the rest of the horoscope should be carefully studied in order to determine the weak points of the constitution).

EXAMPLES

1. Prince Bismarck. ♄ con. ✳ ♅ r. Appointed Prussian Envoy at the Federal Diet in Frankfort.
2. Jay Gould. ♄ con. △ ♅ con. Realised on Kansas Pacific and Union Pacific stocks at a huge profit.
3. Albert Einstein. ♄ con. ⊼ ♅ r. Published his Restricted Theory of Relativity.
4. Colonel Lindbergh. ♄ con. ⊻ ♅ con. Became a Flying Cadet in the Air Service of the War Department. Later made record-breaking Atlantic flight.
5. Karl Marx. ♄ p. □ ♅ r. Tried for High Treason on account of his allegedly seditious newspaper articles. He was acquitted but expelled from Prussia.
6. Karl Marx. ♄ p. □ ♅ p. Son Edgar died.

SATURN—NEPTUNE.

Stimulates the blending of the practical and the idealistic sides of the nature; conscientious devotion to an ideal.

Brings opportunities for gaining advancement through an ability to bring a touch of inspiration to the most prosaic tasks and an aptitude for tackling the most unusual problems in a commonsense and practical manner (Exs. 1 & 2); making progress as a result of a devotion to duty which springs from the native's desire to serve his fellows and causes him to take pleasure in doing work for its own sake or through a desire to please or impress another; bringing plans to a successful conclusion by the exercise of a shrewd foresight which enables him to anticipate any emergency; improving financial position through a sound business sense which enables him to gain through long term investments in concerns connected with oil, shipping, films or drugs.

May denote the development of some psychic faculty; the formation of some friendship, especially with an older person, or a contact with some school of thought which will have a great effect on the native's aims and ideals (the nature of these will depend as much upon his evolutionary status as upon the aspect between the two planets—if he is still bound by the personal limitations of Saturn the contact may indicate that the native lacks a true sense of spiritual values and so becomes attracted towards some form of pseudo-spirituality—if he has risen above these limitations he may be given the opportunity to advance his evolutionary status considerably and to express spiritual ideas in a practical manner so that others less experienced may gain some appreciation of their true value).

Threatens danger of the native becoming entangled in peculiar and involved circumstances (Ex. 3) (even under harmonious aspects) so that he has to negotiate formidable obstacles and to solve knotty problems which require much tedious unravelling before he is finally successful; missing opportunities for advancement through persistently ignoring his intuitions (if Saturn is the stronger) or through a desire to evade responsibility by seeking solitude and retirement (if Neptune is the stronger)—in either case there may be some tendency to develop a false sense of values which may cause him either to neglect his everyday affairs for the sake of some ideal, or to sacrifice his ideals on the altar of ambition; being compelled to submit to frustrating circumstances (he may have to live in a cramped and restricted environment or be forced to undertake unpleasant tasks; his ambitions may be thwarted by events over which he has no control while others may deceive and defraud him or misrepresent his motives and seek to involve him in scandal—such happenings will force him to reflect deeply and, until he has become aware of the illusory nature of the physical world and learned the true meaning of renunciation, he will continue to suffer bitterly as a result of the disappointments which come his way); committing errors of judgment (if Neptune overpowers Saturn) by allowing whims and fancies to override commonsense (in some cases the native will be tempted to act dishonestly in order to further a selfish ambition, through a misplaced and over-shrewd acquisitiveness or as a result of an embittered desire to revenge some real or fancied wrong); incurring losses through unsound investments or as a result of the destruction and deterioration of property (especially through flooding); reduced circumstances (if the contact becomes operative in early life) due to the misfortunes of the father who may be a victim of ill-health, unscrupulous tricksters or his own lack of commonsense; bereavement or the death of the native (in extreme cases).

Affects health through the adverse reaction of an unreasoning pessimism which encourages forebodings of evil, saps the native's resistance to disease in an insidious manner that is hard to detect and hampers the recuperative powers of the body (in order to combat these tendencies the native must fortify his faith, trusting unquestioningly in the ultimate sublimity of his own destiny and remembering that, from a spiritual point of view, all experience is good experience).

EXAMPLES

1. Albert Einstein. $\hbar$ p. $\vee$ Ψ p. Awarded the Nobel Prize for Physics and elected a Member of the Royal Society.
2. Henry Ford. $\hbar$ p. δ Ψ p. Founded the Detroit Motor Company.
3. Madame Blavatsky. $\hbar$ p. $\square$ Ψ r. Attacked by footpads and left in a ditch for dead after being wounded five times. Later, when she was on a sea voyage, the ship

blew up and she lost all her belongings, being left temporarily destitute. She also formed a society for the study of Spiritualism which broke up after a fortnight owing to the fact that several fraudulent mediums imposed upon her and discredited the group.

SATURN—PLUTO.

Stimulates ambition; persistence and perseverance.

(There may be a tendency to display some ruthlessness unless the native has overcome a good deal of the selfish side of Saturn, when he will be likely to show the same unemotional ruthlessness in disciplining his own lower nature. In some cases there will be a tendency towards self-denial and asceticism.)

Brings opportunities for gaining advancement as result of patient, persistent efforts and calm, deliberate actions; achieving ambitions through endurance and enterprise (Exs. 1 & 2) (the native will have the strength and fortitude to behave courageously in the face of adversity).

May denote (in rare cases) the stirring up of suicidal tendencies.

Threatens danger of being subjected to enforced restrictions or made to undergo hardships; setbacks, often as a result of becoming mixed up in extremely involved circumstances (Ex. 3) (unsuspected enemies may work against him in secret or, in extreme cases, he may become the subject of violence, a victim of black magic or fall under a hypnotic spell—sometimes his own harsh behaviour and egotistic outlook may invite retaliation—it will therefore behove the native to pay considerable attention to developing his sympathetic nature, bearing in mind the injunction 'do unto others as you would be done by''); illness or accident involving an older relative (in extreme cases, bereavement or the death of the native himself (Exs. 4 & 5)).

Affects health through troubles involving the teeth and the bony structure of the body; bruises and skin diseases; unusual diseases which may be due to malformations at birth or to the slow and unsuspected accumulation of poisons in the system over a long period (such diseases are often difficult to diagnose and more difficult to cure).

EXAMPLES

1. Annie Besant. ♄ con. ∠ ♀ r. Interests in educational projects aroused. Largely owing to her efforts the Central Hindu College at Benares was built at this time.
2. Prince Bismarck. ♄ con. ∠ ♀ r. Austro-Prussian War. This was one of the final steps in the unification of Germany.
3. Colonel Lindbergh. ♄ con. ⊼ ♀ r. Resigned from the Air Corps following differences of opinion regarding the Second World War.
4. Henry Ford. ♄ p. ⊼ ♀ r. Death.
5. Madame Blavatsky. ♄ p. ⊼ ♀ r. Death.

URANUS—NEPTUNE.

Stimulates idealism; inspirational sensitivity; a desire to experience new sensations (much will depend upon the native's evolutionary status—in some cases the native will give this desire expression by travelling abroad in the physical world in search of fresh and novel experiences—in others, he may seek experience on the emotional plane by attempting to satisfy a restless craving for excitement or novelty or on the mental plane by seeking new philosophies or studying recondite subjects, such as astrology and metaphysics—at the highest level he may strive to develop his intuitive and inspirational faculties by means of meditation, contemplation and similar exercises so that, in rare cases, he will be able to pierce the veil of illusion and so perceive the most prosaic objects in a new and fascinating light).

Brings opportunities for gaining advancement through an ability to combine vision with strength of purpose and through the introduction of an element of novelty into his enterprises; enhancing any powers of artistic inspiration and appreciation as a result of an increased susceptibility to the aesthetic side of life.

May denote a difficulty in achieving a blend between the ideals and the personal desires.

Threatens danger of setbacks due either to a restless craving for excitement or emotional stimulation which may lead the native to indulge in all kinds of unconventional or ill-advised behaviour or to a yearning for independence which may become inflated to such a degree that he will perversely go his own way in the face of all reason (Ex. 1); an inability to bring his enterprises to a successful conclusion as a result of being unable to throw off a vague sense of uncertainty and foreboding which inhibits his actions and fails to inspire the confidence of potential allies; a dissipation of psychic energy in some form of pseudo-religious devotion, in artistic activities of a bohemian or eccentric nature or in some path of service which is either unworthy of his attention or in which his ideas are carried to extremes (sometimes the native may be driven into perverse and foolish actions by the compelling urge of what appears to be the voice of conscience—it will pay him to seek the counsel of those wiser and more mature than himself, for his plans, however well-intentioned, have a habit of misfiring and creating the opposite effect to that intended; if he is not well balanced, his moodiness and erratic tendencies may encourage neurotic susceptibilities or, in extreme cases, lead him into ways of dissipation or vice) bereavement (Exs. 2 & 3) (especially the loss of a friend of long standing) or the death of the native himself (Ex. 4) (no major catastrophe need be feared unless other strong progressed afflictions are in force).

Affects health through diseases which develop as a result of hereditary weaknesses in the system or through displaced, inverted, enlarged or atrophied organs (manipulative or electrical methods of treatment often prove to be most successful); the after effects of a period of severe nervous strain (Ex. 3) during which neurotic complaints may develop (if such tendencies are suggested by the nativity).

(The native should take particular care if he wishes to indulge in any occult or mystical experiments as unwholesome entities may be attracted into his aura and he may become liable to obsession.)

EXAMPLES

1. Annie Besant. ♅ r. ∠ ♆ con. Interned by the British authorities in India during the first World War. Her activities on behalf of the campaign for Indian Home Rule were deemed to be an obstruction to the war effort.
2. Mary Baker Eddy. ♅ con. ☌ ♆ r. Married. After six months her husband died. Three months later a son was born.

3. Ralph Waldo Emerson. ♅ r. ∠ ♆ con. First wife died. Retired from his office as pastor deeply depressed in health and spirits.
4. Cecil Rhodes. ♅ p. ⚹ ♆ p. Death.

URANUS—PLUTO.

Stimulates desires for independence and freedom; originality and powers of invention.

Brings opportunities for making discoveries as a result of painstaking and thorough researches in some particular field—such discoveries are rendered the more effective through the native's ability to combine the methods of others and add to them some distinctive factor of his own; gaining advancement as a result of inventive, scientific or technical abilities, pioneering spirit, power of independent action, and an ability to act suddenly at the most opportune moment; group leadership of a dynamic kind (success in activities of this nature will largely hinge upon a faculty for understanding group psychology and a genius for persuasively exploiting his own personality).

May denote a period when the native is able to make much progress in developing spiritual insight and intuition (Ex. 1) (much will depend upon the evolutionary status of the native—in any case there should be an increased ability to reach conclusions by means of a flash of inspiration rather than by more orthodox methods).

Threatens danger of arousing strong opposition as a result of acting in too eccentric or self-willed a manner—in extreme cases the native may be tempted to take the law into his own hands, a course of action which may be attended by disastrous results! (Ex. 2) (sometimes an unreasoning fanaticism or a blind zeal will make it difficult for the native to behave in a logical or orthodox manner—he should realize that he is more likely to gain his ends by persuasion than by coercion and should meditate upon the prayer, "Thy Will be done", endeavouring to cultivate a calm and patient resignation to the impact of events, however difficult this may be); bereavement (Exs. 3 & 4) or death of the native (Exs. 5 & 6) (in rare cases suicidal tendencies may be stimulated or death may occur suddenly in strange circumstances).

Promotes good health through increased vitality.

Affects health through accidents involving electrical apparatus or machinery; paralysis; nervous breakdown or insanity (no major catastrophe need be feared unless other strong progressed afflictions are also operative).

Examples

(In view of the small number of times exact aspects between Uranus and Pluto are formed in the example horoscopes, aspects made jointly to both bodies by the progressed angles are also included for purposes of illustration.)

1. Ralph Waldo Emerson. Asc. con. ⊻ ♅ r. △ ♇ r. Attended Cambridge Divinity School.
2. Adolf Hitler. M.C. p. ∠ ♅ r. □ ♇ r. Ringleader of the ill-fated "Bavaria Putsch".
3. Adolf Hitler. M.C. con. □ ♅ r. ∠ ♇ r. Father died.
4. Ralph Waldo Emerson. M.C. p. ☌ ♅ r. ⊼ ♇ r. Wife died.
5. Madame Blavatsky. ♅ p. ⚹ ♇ r. Death.
6. Adolf Hitler. M.C. con. ⚼ ♅ r. ☌ ♇ r. Death.

NEPTUNE—PLUTO.

Stimulates a desire to transcend all boundaries, often through the intensification of emotional experience—(Much will depend upon the native's evolutionary status and upon the general tenor of the nativity. In some cases, a craving to feel at one with the world may express itself through artistic endeavours or an interest in mysticism which may lead, at the highest level to a sensitive awareness of the superphysical worlds. This sensitivity may be developed through the practice of meditation and contemplation. In other cases, especially when the native has not acquired a fair measure of moral, mental and emotional stability, there may be a restless search for the unusual and the weird); idealism as a means of regeneration. (The native will always be conscious of some great ideal which he will strive ceaselessly to attain. His efforts to reach this ideal may take him far afield and lead him through many strange experiences.)

Brings opportunities for gaining advancement as a result of a clear-sighted and intuitive approach to the world which may range from great spiritual understanding to an uncanny ability in everyday life to perceive the true motives of others and to play upon their susceptibilities, according to the general condition of the nativity (Exs. 1 & 2) (in exceptional cases this quality, coupled with an enhanced personal magnetism, will enable him to develop the power to influence large masses of people); undertaking extensive travels often as a result of a restless desire to expand his horizons; joining in group activities connected with charitable works as a means of developing and expanding the emotions.

May denote the taking up of most extraordinary activities under the spur of an imagination capable of touching the sublimest heights or the lowest depths; a tendency for the native to be drawn into very mysterious and obscure circumstances so that he is faced with knotty and intricate problems, the unravelling of which will demand the utmost perspicacity and the most thorough-going perseverance; a yearning for self-purification which, combined with an inner realization of the necessity to practise renunciation, can lead to considerable self-discipline and self-denial (in rare cases the native may attain spiritual regeneration through completely loosing hold upon the bodily appetites, through a selfless resignation to the Will of God and a thorough-going renunciation of any desire to benefit through the exploitation of even the most defenceless of God's creatures).

Threatens danger of setbacks resulting from some basic instability of character (the native may be hopelessly idealistic or completely unpractical so that he fails to manage his affairs in a businesslike manner or he may completely lack ideals and so conduct himself without the slightest regard for morality—in extreme cases he may sink into such a morass of base and perverted iniquity that he becomes overwhelmed by his animal nature and thus moved to commit deeds of a most debauched and brutal character); being unable to inspire the confidence of those around him as a result of some subtle defect in his personal magnetism—in some cases he may arouse their open antagonism (Ex. 3) or, worse still, their secret hostility—thus he may always have some cross to bear; being deceived and led astray by unworthy companions and being beset by all manner of temptations, many of which he will no recognise as such until it is too late to avert the consequences (this will be a severe testing time when the native will be placed in circumstances designed to search out and probe the chinks in his spiritual armour—the slightest moral obliquity or blind spot in his spiritual awareness may then cause him to lose all the fruits of his labours so that he will ever have reason to remember the Achilles' heel that proved to be his undoing—if, on the other hand, his conduct is above suspicion his actions may be completely misinterpreted and his motives twisted and distorted so that his most self-sacrificing gestures and noblest deeds are misunderstood and maliciously misrepresented); bereavement (Exs. 4 & 5) or death of the native (Exs. 6 & 7) (or he may disappear under mysterious circumstances or fall seriously ill or suffer from some obsession—in rare cases he may practise or become the victim of black magic, or suicidal tendencies may be stimulated if the native shows tendencies towards rashness, over-sensitivity and self-abnegation coupled with a lack of moral fibre).

Affects health through the extreme sensitivity of the constitution—a comparatively minor ailment can have deep and far-reaching effects (through the same sensitivity warning symptoms of trouble may arise at an early stage and so enable the native to take timely measures to eradicate the ailment); an extreme susceptibility to drugs (the system is apt to react violently to any impurity and therefore the native will be liable to suffer from various kinds of poisoning—he should be especially careful in the use of drugs and should reduce his intake of alcohol and avoid all stale, contaminated or over-ripe food); a deep-seated and unreasoning feeling of terror (in some instances) that no amount of persuasion can allay, which lowers the vitality and encourages the onset of all kinds of disabilities and neurotic complaints; contact with noxious gases; the over-sensitivity of the native's superphysical vehicles (hostile entities may invade his aura or ill-conceived experiments may upset the alignment of his finer bodies with disastrous results).

EXAMPLES

(In view of the small number of times exact aspects between Neptune and Pluto are formed in the example horoscopes, aspects made jointly to both bodies by the progressed angles are used for purposes of illustration.)

1. Prince Bismarck. M.C. p. ☍ Ψ r. □ ♀ r. Appointed Minister President of Prussia.
2. Mary Baker Eddy. Asc. p. □ Ψ r. ☌ ♀ r. Organised the First Church of Christ, Scientist, in order to gain greater control of the movement. At the same time she strengthened her propaganda machine by founding the Christian Science Publishing Society. She also moved to a new headquarters.
3. Prince Bismarck. M.C. con. ⚹ Ψ r. ⊻ ♀ r. Resigned Chancellorship of the German Reich.
4. Prince Bismarck. Asc. con. ☍ Ψ r. □ ♀ r. Wife and brother died. He was seriously ill.
5. Mary Baker Eddy. M.C. p. □ Ψ r. ☍ ♀ r. Married. After six months her husband died. Three months later a son was born.
6. Adolf Hitler. Asc. p. ☍ midpoint Ψ ♀ r. Died.
7. Karl Marx. Asc. p. ☍ Ψ p. □ ♀ con. Died from lung trouble.

CUSPAL DIRECTIONS

Just as the Midheaven and Ascendant of the radical figure progress through the Zodiac when directed, it follows also that the intermediate house cusps must move proportionately and, in so doing, form aspects with the radical and progressed planets. While it is not advisable to base conclusions solely on the evidence of an aspect between a progressed intermediate cusp and a planet, directions formed in this manner are sometimes valuable as corroborative evidence. When the signs corresponding to a certain house or when the rulers of that house are prominently involved by progression, any aspects formed by the progressed cusp of that house, or by a progressed planet to the radical cusp, assume greater importance and increase the probability that events will take place of the nature of the house concerned. It is unwise to pay too much importance to this type of direction if strong major directions are not operative at the same time.

It is not proposed to list the effects caused by the various planets in aspect with each separate house cusp since readers should now be familiar with the general influence of the planets for good or ill and with the general significance of each house.

It will be obvious that an aspect involving the cusp of the Second House will also involve the cusp of the Eighth, while one involving the Third House cusp will also involve the Ninth cusp, and so on. It will not always be easy, therefore, to narrow down the field in which an intermediate cuspal aspect is likely to operate unless a thorough study of the major directions in force has first been made.

The following illustrations of intermediate cuspal directions, taken from the example horoscopes on pages 147–149, provide ample evidence of the efficacy of this class of direction:—

SECOND HOUSE CUSP

Jay Gould. Cusp 2 p. △ ☉ r. Sold Kansas Pacific stock at huge profit. Cusp 2 r. ☌ ☉ p. ☌ ♀ r. Sold Union Pacific stock at huge profit.
Prince Bismarck. Cusp 2 con. △ ☉ p. △ ♃ p. Received a large gift of money for Services to Germany. Purchased estate.
Madame Blavatsky. Cusp 2 r. ☌ ♂ con. Ship on which she was travelling blown up. Temporarily destitute. (♂ r. in Third House ☌ ♄.)
Albert Einstein. Cusp 2 con. □ ☉ r. Won Nobel Prize for Physics, £10,000. Gave it all to charity. (☉ r. in ♓.)
Karl Marx. Cusp 2 p. ☌ ☉ p. □ ♄ con. Began a period of hardship. (☉ r. eclipsed in ♉.) Cusp 2 p. ☍ ♅ r. Was bequeathed a small legacy.

THIRD HOUSE CUSP

Annie Besant. Cusp 3 con. ☌ ♅ r. ☍ ☿ r. Interest in education aroused. Helped to establish Central Hindu College at Benares. Cusp 3 con. ☌ ♂ r. Joined staff of the *National Reformer*. Spent year touring and lecturing. Cusp 3 con. ☌ ♀ r. Sailed for New York. Recalled almost immediately following the death of Madame Blavatsky.
Prince Bismarck. Cusp 3 p. □ ♀ r. Death of brother. (♀ in Eighth House □ ♆ r.)
Madame Blavatsky. Cusp 3 p. ☌ ☽ r. ☍ ♀ r. Cusp 3 con. ☍ ♆ r. Wrote *Isis Unveiled*
Albert Einstein. Cusp 3 p. ☌ ♅ r. Ran away from school to join parents in Italy A year's break in education.
Ralph Waldo Emerson. Cusp 3 con. ☍ ☉ r. Honorary LL.D. degree conferred on him by Harvard University. (☉ r. in ♊.)
Karl Marx. Cusp 3 con. ☌ ☉ r. Studied at Bonn University. Cusp 3 p. ☍ ♅ r. Switched from Bonn to Berlin University. (♅ in ♐.) Cusp 3 p. ☍ ♆ r. □ ♀ r. Resigned editorship of newspaper. Removed to Paris.

FIFTH HOUSE CUSP

Annie Besant. Cusp 5 p. ☍ ♅ r. ☌ ☿ r. Sued for the return of Krishnamurti and his brother whom she had formally adopted.

Prince Bismarck. Cusp 5 p. △ ♀ r. Engaged twice in one year. (♀ culminates.) Cusp 5 r. ☌ ♂ con. Interfered in son's love affair.

Mary Baker Eddy. Cusp 5 r. ☌ ♂ con. Son moved to West. Many years' separation followed. Cusp 5 r. ☌ ♀ con. Adopted a son.

Jay Gould. Cusp 5 con. ✶ ♃ con. Son born. Cusp 5 con. ☍ ♅ r. Daughter born.

Anne Morrow Lindbergh. Cusp 5 con. ☍ ☽ ♂ ♆ r. ☌ ♅ con. Child kidnapped and murdered. Cusp 5 con. ☌ ♅ r. Second child born.

Colonel Charles Lindbergh. Cusp 5 con. □ ☽ r. Cusp 5 p. □ ☉ r. First child born.

SIXTH HOUSE CUSP

Prince Bismarck. Cusp 6 p. ☌ ♀ p. Gravely ill. (♀ r. in ♓.)

Ralph Waldo Emerson. Cusp 6 p. ☍ ♆ r. Threatened consumption. (♆ r. rises ☌ Asc. r.)

Cecil Rhodes. Cusp 6 con. ☌ ♄ p. Health broke down. Cusp 6 con. ☌ ♄ con. Consumption. Given six months to live!

EIGHTH HOUSE CUSP

Annie Besant. Cusp 8 p. ☌ ♃ r. Death.

Prince Bismarck. Cusp 8 r. ☌ ♂ p. Franco-German War. Cusp 8 con. ☌ ♂ r. Attempted assassination. Cusp 8 p. □ ♂ p. Death.

Ralph Waldo Emerson. Cusp 8 r. □ ♂ p. Death.

Karl Marx. Cusp 8 p. □ ♄ p. Son Edgar died.

NINTH HOUSE CUSP

Madame Blavatsky. Cusp 9 p. ✶ ♅ r. Cusp 9 con. ☌ ♆ r. Travelled to India.

Albert Einstein. Cusp 9 r. ☌ ☉ con. ☌ ♃ con. Appointed to Chair of Research at University of Berlin. A congenial change from lecturing. Cusp 9 con. △ ♅ r. Professor of Mathematics at Princeton University. Made home in U.S.A. (♅ rules Ninth House.)

Anne Morrow Lindbergh. Cusp 9 p. ☌ ♀ r. Made home in England.

Colonel Charles Lindbergh. Cusp 9 p. ☍ ☉ p. ☿ r. Made home in England. Cusp 9 con. ☍ ☉ con. ♄ r. Flew Atlantic.

Karl Marx. Cusp 9 p. △ ☽ r. Returned to the Continent for a visit after making his home in England.

ELEVENTH HOUSE CUSP

Albert Einstein. Cusp 11 con. ☌ ♃ r. Awarded Nobel Prize for Physics. Cusp 11 con. □ ♀ r. Friend Dr. Rathenau assassinated. (♀ r. in Eleventh House; cusp 11 con. in ♒.) Cusp 11 con. ☌ ♅ con. Friend Adler sentenced to death for having killed Premier of Austria. He was later reprieved.

Karl Marx. Cusp 11 p. ☍ ♂ ♌ p. First met Engels, one of his few real friends.

TWELFTH HOUSE CUSP

Adolf Hitler. Cusp 12 p. ☍ ☉ r. Cusp 12 con. □ ♆ ♀ r. Imprisoned after "Bavaria Putsch."

Karl Marx. Cusp 12 p. ☌ ♄ con. Cusp 12 con. ☌ ♆ r. □ ♀ r. Tried for High Treason.

Cecil Rhodes. Cusp 12 con. ☍ ♅ con. Besieged in Kimberley during Boer War.

Chapter VIII

FINAL HINTS ON THE JUDGMENT OF YEARLY SECONDARY DIRECTIONS

IT is a comparatively easy matter to estimate the probable effect of a single progressed aspect but when several directions of differing natures fall due in one year, as they are apt to do if events of great importance are scheduled to take place, judgment becomes more difficult. Unless the student is experienced in correlating the various angular, solar, interplanetary and cuspal directions, he is likely to find himself confronted with the task of choosing between several possible interpretations of the directions in force.

When formulating a judgment it is necessary to bear in mind that some events will have repercussions on more than one department of the life, consequently several planets, signs and houses may be involved simultaneously. Marriage, for instance, is not only a matter concerning the Seventh House, for, at such a time, the native usually sets up a home of his own (Fourth House) and acquires a group of relatives-in-law (Ninth House); sometimes he moves away from his old companions, forming new friendships (Eleventh House) and he often finds that his financial position is considerably modified (Second House). Some of these events will be denoted by favourable and others by unfavourable aspects, although all will come about as a result of one single main event. Other major happenings in the life will have similarly widespread effects, involving several sectors of the chart at the same time.

It is therefore necessary first to distinguish between those directions which indicate major events and those which denote the less important happenings arising out of these major events. As emphasized in Chapter III, no happening of real importance comes to pass unheralded by directions involving the Midheaven or the Ascendant. Often, both types of direction will be operative at this time. The planet, or pair or group of planets which is in aspect to the angles will provide a very strong indication of the type of event that may be anticipated. It has been demonstrated in Chapter V that the effect of a planet in the progressed horoscope must be considered not only in relation to its sign and house position, both radical and progressed, but also in relation to the aspects which it receives from other planets. The house or houses which it rules must also be taken into account. Progressed planets in conjunction with the Midheaven and Ascendant or in opposition or in square to these angles, operate with the greatest potency. In this respect it should be remembered that aspects formed between progressed angles and converse planets and between converse angles and progressed planets have as much bearing upon the fortunes of the native as any other angular direction.

When several different and apparently equally probable solutions present themselves, these may be narrowed down by referring firstly to any solar directions in force. These directions are nearly always potent in their effects, and the nature of the planet in aspect to the Sun, as well as the Sun's sign and house position and house rulership, will often provide very useful corroboration of some outstanding trend indicated by an angular direction. Reference should then be made to the interplanetary aspects in force. It will often be found that one planet is particularly prominent, forming aspects both by its progressed and converse motion and receiving aspects to its radical position from other progressed or converse planets. In such a case this planet will prove a strong pointer to the department of life most likely to be affected.

When several planets are equally prominent in the year's directions, the relative strength of the planets in the nativity will furnish a clue as to which is likely to produce the most far-reaching effects by progression. Those planets which are angular are likely to exert the strongest influence; those which receive several close aspects are the next important, while those placed in their own signs will also act with noticeable effect.

When judging the relative strength of directions, it should be remembered that an aspect formed between a progressed angle and a progressed planet, or between two progressed planets, is often no less potent in its effects than a similar aspect involving a radical angle or planet. It should also be noted that there is no difference in effect between progressed and converse positions. Both are likely to act with equal power, although converse directions seem to coincide more frequently with important events than do progressed directions. If, as suggested in Chapter I, progressed directions bear a special relationship to events which the native has attracted to himself as a result of exercising his free will in his present incarnation, while converse directions are particularly connected with events arising out of causes set in motion by the native in former lives, it would appear from this evidence that the majority of mankind are still mainly concerned with the working off of past karmic debts.

However powerful interplanetary aspects may appear to be, their effects are less potent than those of angular and solar directions except in cases where one of the planets is also the ruler of the Ascendant. Even when the testimony of the interplanetary aspects seems to override that of the angular or solar directions in force, the trends indicated by the two latter classes of aspect must always be given pride of place when forming the final judgment.

Finally, a scrutiny should be made of any directions involving the intermediate house cusps. In the writer's experience, the Placidean system of house division gives the best results in this connection. Cuspal directions generally operate most powerfully when a planet comes by progression to the cusp of the house which it occupied at birth. The affairs governed by that house will then assume a more than usual prominence in the native's life and the cuspal directions will thus emphasize the importance of other directions in force which involve the house or the corresponding sign.

When assessing the probable action of directions always bear in mind the Golden Rule—that nothing can come to pass under the stimulus of progressed aspects which is not foreshadowed in the birth map. This does not mean that aspects formed after birth between planets which were not in aspect in the nativity will have little or no effect, but that they will probably have a less pronounced effect than progressed aspects formed between planets which were already in aspect with each other in the nativity.

It is a good plan to make a note of the particular events that occurred earlier in the native's life under previous planetary configurations of a nature similar to those under consideration, for it often happens that an event which coincides with the culmination of one progressed aspect is later modified by a second event occurring at the time of a subsequent progressed aspect between the same two bodies.

For instance, Mary Baker Eddy married for the second time when the progressed Venus was in opposition to the converse Uranus. Her husband was sent to prison when the progressed Venus reached the square of the progressed Uranus and he later deserted her when the progressed Venus arrived at the square of the radical Uranus. Ralph Waldo Emerson married when the progressed Mars was in square to the radical Neptune. His wife died three years later when the converse Mars reached the trine of the radical Neptune. Prince Bismarck was appointed Minister President of Prussia when the progressed Midheaven was in opposition to the radical Neptune and in square to the radical Pluto. He finally resigned from power when the converse Midheaven reached the sextile of the radical Neptune and the quincunx of the radical Pluto.

Not only is it essential to establish the main trend of a group of directions but it is also necessary to decide whether the directions are preponderantly benefic or malefic. If the majority of the directions over a period of several years is unfavourable, the native is likely to become less and less able to withstand their impact, especially in so far as his health is concerned. By observing the character of directions over a period of several years it will then be possible to determine the time when the nature of the directions changes perceptibly from favourable to unfavourable, or vice versa. It is thus possible to forecast when the native is likely to experience a drastic change of fortune.

The effects of directions are not always immediately noticeable in the native's outer life and it is therefore unwise to assume too hastily that a certain direction has failed to produce appropriate results. The seeds of some future action may be sown under the stimulus of a direction but the harvest may not be reaped for many years. In this connection it should be noted that enterprises set in motion under favourable directions will ultimately flourish, however belatedly, while commitments entered into under unfavourable directions must ultimately work out to the native's disadvantage. A typical example of the delayed action of directions is furnished in the life of Adolf Hitler, who first became obsessed with the idea of regenerating Germany at the age of thirty, when the progressed Midheaven formed a trine with the radical Sun. He did not enjoy any exceptional preferment at this time, but the stimulus of this idea was ultimately the mainspring of his spectacular rise to power. As the progressed Midheaven was simultaneously afflicted by a square from the radical Neptune, his obsession finally proved to be the cause of his own undoing and was the indirect source of sorrow and suffering for millions of his fellow men.

The following examples of the judgment of Yearly Directions are given in order to illustrate the practical application of the principles outlined above. (In order to determine the actual time when the directions are likely to operate it is necessary to consider the monthly, weekly and daily series of progressions which fall due during the same period. This branch of prediction is dealt with in subsequent chapters.)

The first example concerns the directions in Annie Besant's chart when she was seven years old. They were as follows:—

M.C.p. ☍ ☽ r. ☿ p. △ ♆ r.
M.C. con. ⚹ ♆ r.
M.C. r. □ ☿ con.

There are, of course, only a limited number of events which can happen in the life of a seven-year-old child, whose affairs at this time will normally be closely bound up with those of the parents. Annie Besant's father had died when she was five and her younger brother had died a year later. Her mother had moved house after this second bereavement.

The task is simplified in this instance by the fact that only three planets, Moon, Mercury and Neptune, are involved in the year's directions. The Moon and Mercury are pre-eminently the planets of change, being unstable by nature. Furthermore, in the birth chart, the radical Mercury in Libra is in square to the radical Moon, forming two of the arms of a T-square with the radical Uranus. The Moon, the general significator of the domestic circumstances, is in the domestic sign Cancer in the Fourth House and is also the ruler of that house, thus placing a fourfold emphasis on the home environment and, in particular, on the mother. Therefore we can confidently predict a change in the domestic circumstances. As the radical Moon is afflicted, although in conjunction with Jupiter, the probability of an unfavourable change is suggested. The converse Mercury also takes with it the impress of the radical opposition to Uranus, so that its square to the radical Midheaven implies a rather sudden and enforced change.

Neptune in the nativity is not strongly aspected but is placed in the Twelfth House, the house of restrictions and sorrows, in square to the cusp of the Second House, the house governing material resources. The main trend of the directions therefore suggests that this change in the domestic environment is likely to prove a frustrating experience for the young child.

What actually happened was that her mother gave up the house in which they were living, owing to straitened financial circumstances, and took her to live in lodgings at Harrow, a step made easier by the fact that the numbers of the family had been depleted during the two previous years.

The following directions were operative in Adolf Hitler's chart when he was thirteen:—

M.C. p. ☌ ♄ r. ☉ p. □ ♄ r. ☿ r. ⚺ ♂ p.
M.C. con. □ ♅ r. ☉ con. ☍ ♅ r. & p. (separating)
Asc. r. ⚻ ♂ p.
Asc. con. ⚼ ♆ r. 8th cusp p. ☌ ♆ r.

The only technically favourable aspect is the semi-sextile between the progressed Mars and the radical Mercury. As the radical Mars is in detriment and is in square to Saturn in its fall, little good is likely to result from directions involving Mars. Having discounted the power for good of this aspect we now find ourselves confronted with an unrelieved battery of formidable afflictions, in which Saturn and Uranus figure most prominently.

Saturn, elevated in the Tenth House, and Uranus are the joint rulers of the fourth House and both planets are involved in afflictions to the Sun, the Tenth House ruler. This prominence of the Fourth and Tenth Houses focuses attention upon family matters and the domestic environment and in particular upon the affairs of the father, for the Sun and Saturn are the general significators of the male parent. The radical Saturn is afflicted by Mars, and the radical Uranus is in sesquiquadrate to Pluto in the Eighth House, the house of death. The ominous import of these directions now becomes plainer. The quincunx between the progressed Mars and the radical Ascendant, together with the conjunction of the radical Neptune and the progressed Eighth cusp, and the sesquiquadrate between the converse Ascendant and the radical Neptune in the Eighth House, show clearly the threat of bereavement.

Hitler's father died at this time and the event must have brought to the surface all his latent desires for self-expression and independent action. Not only was Uranus rising in the nativity with Pluto, the planet of intensification, in aspect to it, but Saturn was in Leo, while Mercury in the sign of leadership was stimulated by the semi-sextile from the progressed Mars. The financial hardship caused by this bereavement is shown in the directions by the prominence of Saturn, which is afflicted in the nativity by Mars, the ruler of the Second House, in Taurus, the second sign. The conjunction of the progressed eighth cusp with Neptune is a further significator of financial difficulties.

The final example is taken from the horoscope of Ann Harding. When she was twenty-four the following directions were in operation:—

Asc. r. △ ♀ p.	☉ r. ♂ ♀ p.	♀ con. △ ♃ con.
Asc. r. ☍ ♀ con.	☉ p. ⊻ ☽ r.	☿ p. △ ♄ con.
(applying)	☉ con. ☍ ♄ p.	♀ con. ☍ ♅ r.
Asc. con △ ♂ p.	☉ r. ☍ ♃ con.	
M.C. r. ✶ ♂ p.		
M.C. p. □ ☉ con.		

Two contacts between Venus and the Ascendant place a strong emphasis on romance, especially as Venus is connected with the Ascendant by quincunx aspect in the nativity. In addition, the radical Venus is in conjunction with Mars, so that the contacts between the progressed Mars and the radical Midheaven and converse Ascendant are also coloured to a certain extent by the Venusian rays. As the Sun is in trine to the Ascendant in the natal chart, the arrival of the progressed Venus at the conjunction of the Sun is a most important direction. The progressed Sun is in semisextile to the radical Moon in Libra, the sign of marriage, while Mercury, the ruler of the corresponding Seventh House, has progressed to the trine of the converse

Saturn. In addition, the converse Sun in the domestic sign Cancer is in square to the progressed Midheaven in Libra.

The great activity of Venus, coupled with the equally prominent solar aspects, places a strong emphasis on the possibility of marriage. The Sun is a general signifi-cator of the husband in a woman's chart and its contact with the Moon by progres-sion is an aspect typical of marriage, especially as the radical Moon is in Libra. The Martian contacts also suggest that the opposite sex is likely to play a greater part in her life at this time.

Under these aspects Ann Harding did, in fact, marry but the marriage was eventually dissolved. It will be noticed that the only technically adverse aspects in operation at the time were those between the Sun and Saturn and between Venus and Uranus. There were, however, more serious afflictions in the radical chart. The seventh cusp was close to Pluto and in opposition to Uranus; Neptune and Mars in the Seventh House were squared by the Moon in Libra, while Venus was in opposition to Saturn, in quincunx to Uranus and in conjunction with Mars.

Chapter IX

THE MONTHLY SERIES OF SECONDARY DIRECTIONS

AT this stage it is appropriate to introduce a completely new item of astrological technique, the day-for-a-month-series of progressions. In Chapter I was expressed the view that, since the True Solar Day could successfully be equated to one year, there seemed to be no logical reason why the same symbolic unit of time should not be equated to recognised units of time that were shorter than a year in duration. The year is a natural time unit, based upon the Earth's orbital revolution round the Sun. As all calculations in Geocentric astrology are based on the planets' apparent motion in relation to the Earth, we regard the Sun as the moving body, and not the Earth. Thus, in any given one year period, the Sun will appear, from the point of view of an observer standing on the Earth's surface, to travel through the twelve signs of the Zodiac, returning once more to its original position at the end of the year. This fact demonstrates that the twelve calendar months, although not coinciding exactly with the Sun's entry into the signs of the moveable Zodiac, are nevertheless based on a particular relationship between the Sun and the Earth. Since the True Solar Day also depends upon a Sun-Earth relationship, as explained in Chapter II, it will be seen that there is a common factor in the determination of both measures of time, which brings about a sympathetic relationship between them.

A chart cast each year for the Sun's entry into the sign Aries is held to be of special significance in judging the events of the following year. This is because the Sun carries with it a special charge of energy which is infused anew into the Zodiac every time the Sun recommences its annual zodiacal journey. Similar charts set up for the entry of the Sun into Cancer, Libra and Capricorn are held to have an almost equal significance. Some astrologers base their predictions on horoscopes cast for the monthly entry of the Sun into each zodiacal sign. In genethliacal astrology the yearly return of the Sun to the place in the Zodiac that it held at birth corresponds to its entry into Aries in the mundane sphere. Such a figure, drawn up for the moment of the Sun's return to its radical position in any chart, is known as a Solar Revolution. Drawing a parallel from the mundane sphere it would appear valid to cast a chart for the Sun's arrival at a point 30, 60, 90 degrees, and so on, away from its radical position, such charts coinciding with the mundane figures set up for the Sun's ingress into Taurus, Gemini, Cancer, and so on. It will be seen, therefore, that there are good grounds for regarding any yearly period as being divisible into twelve equal parts, measured on the basis of the Sun's progress through the Zodiac.

The twelve-fold division of the Zodiac corresponds to the twelve formative forces of nature, known to occultists. The twelve tribes of Israel, the twelve gates of the New Jerusalem, the twelve precious stones in the breastplate of the High Priest and the twelve disciples are well-known biblical references to the potent significance of the number twelve. It will thus be apparent that the existence of twelve Zodiacal signs and of twelve months in the year is no mere accident but has a deep mystic significance, being the reflection in the mundane sphere of a great natural law.

In order to calculate the day-for-a-month progressions measuring to any given period of the life the same method as that used in determining the day-for-a-year series should be employed, except that instead of counting one day backwards and forwards from the day of birth for each year of life, twelve days are now taken to represent this period. Periods of less than a year can easily be equated to the appropriate number of days. In order to facilitate the calculation of the exact number of days equivalent to any year of the life by this measure it will be found convenient to use the tables in Appendix I.

The Midheaven of the monthly progressed chart moves forward by an amount corresponding to the distance travelled by the Sun between the day of birth and the directional day which measures to the month under review. The converse monthly Midheaven moves backward through the Zodiac by an amount corresponding to the distance travelled by the Sun between the day of birth and the directional day before birth which measures to the month under review. It will thus be appreciated that the rate of progress of the monthly Midheaven is approximately 12 degrees per year.

Aspects between the natal planets and angles and the progressed and converse monthly planets and angles are tabulated in exactly the same way as the aspects occurring in the yearly series of progressions. Not only should the progressed and converse charts be compared with the nativity, but they should also be carefully dovetailed with each other to form a completely integrated whole. The power of the directions formed by this intermediate rate of progression is naturally less than that of the yearly progressions but their influence is nevertheless considerable. The slow-moving planets often remain within close orbs of an aspect for whole months at a time, thus casting their influence over a lengthy period. Particular attention should be paid to the periods when progressed monthly planets form strong aspects with the angles of the radical chart or with the angles of the progressed and converse yearly charts. Aspects between the positions of progressed monthly planets and progressed yearly planets should also be carefully watched. Apart from their connection with the radical chart and the day-for-a-year series of progressions, however, progressed monthly charts are often significant in themselves. Once again, it is the aspects between the moving planets and the progressed and converse angles of the monthly charts which are of primary importance in determining vital periods in the life.

The following is an example of the calculation of Monthly Secondary Progressions. It is required to ascertain the monthly directions in force in the horoscope of Ann Harding (data given on page 17) during October, 1926:—

Date of birth. . . . . .7th August, 1902
Month for which directions are required. .October, 1926
Number of years and months after day of birth. . . . . .24 years 2 months
= 290 months

290 days after birth....................................24th May, 1903
290 days before birth..............................21st October, 1901
    (A Table simplifying the calculation of directional days before and after birth in the Monthly Series of progressions is provided in Appendix I.)

Calculation of Progressed Monthly Midheaven:—

Sun's position at noon on 24th May, 1903		2° ♊ 08′
Sun's position at noon on day of birth		14° ♌ 02′
Difference	9 signs	18° 06′
Position of radical Midheaven		27° ♍ 39′
*Add difference between Sun positions	9 signs	18° 06′
Position of Progressed Monthly Midheaven		15° ♋ 45′

By referring to the Tables of Houses for 29°N.47′ we find that the Ascendant corresponding to this Midheaven is.................. 14° ♎ 05′

The Converse Monthly Midheaven is calculated as follows:—

Sun's position at noon on day of birth		14° ♌ 02′
Sun's position at noon on 21st October, 1901		27° ♎ 24′
Difference	9 signs	16° 38′
Position of radical Midheaven		27° ♍ 39′
*Subtract difference between Sun positions	9 signs	16° 38′
Position of Converse Monthly Midheaven		11° ♐ 01′

By referring to the Tables of Houses for 29°N.47′ we find that the Ascendant corresponding to this Midheaven is............... 0° ♓ 54′

All that remains now is to tabulate the aspects formed between the various radical, progressed and converse angles and planets in the same manner as for Yearly Secondary Directions, with this important addition, that special care and attention should be paid to any progressed or converse monthly planets aspecting the progressed or converse yearly angles or the angles of the birth chart.

Generally speaking, there is little to be gained by making use of the aspects formed by the progressed monthly Moon. As twenty-four hours represent the space

*(N.B.—In cases where a subtraction has to be made and the difference is in excess of six signs, it will often be found more convenient to *add* the complementary part of the Zodiac instead of deducting the larger part; similarly, when an addition has to be made, it is often easier to *subtract* the complementary portion of the Zodiac.)

of one month, a day is represented by the passage of less than an hour. Each degree of the Moon's progress in the Zodiac, therefore, represents about two and a half days. The time at which monthly directions are most likely to discharge their effects can be established with greater precision by bringing into play the weekly and daily series of directions rather than by relying upon the progress of the monthly Moon.

In the case under consideration the following are the monthly directions:—

M.C. p. ☌ ♀ r.   ☉ p. ⊼ ♆ r.   ♀ p. ☌ ♂ r.
M.C. r. ☌ ♂ p. (operative over many   ♃ p. ☐ ♀ r.
                              months)   ♄ p. ☌ ♃ p.
M.C. con. ☌ ♀ con. (separating)   (in yearly series)
M.C. r. ⊼ ☉ con.   ☿ con. △ ♃ p.
Asc. p. ✶ ☉ r. ☌ ☊ p.   ♀ con. △ ☿ r.
Asc. r. ☍ ☿ p.

We have examined, in the previous chapter, the yearly secondary directions under which Ann Harding came to marry at this time. A study of the above monthly directions shows beyond any shadow of doubt that this was the one period of the year when the influences indicating marriage reached their peak. The progressed monthly Midheaven had reached the place of Venus in the nativity; the converse monthly Midheaven had been travelling in conjunction with the converse Venus, which at this time completed its trine with the radical Mercury, the ruler of the Seventh House.

Further testimonies of marriage are the sextile between the progressed monthly Ascendant in Libra and the radical Sun, the semi-sextile between the converse monthly Sun in Libra and the radical Midheaven, the opposition between the progressed monthly Mercury, the ruler of the Seventh House, and the radical Ascendant, and the conjunction of the progressed monthly Venus and the radical Mars.

Had this particular group of monthly directions been in force at a time when no major directions indicative of marriage were in operation, there would hardly have been any justification for predicting that marriage would then take place. But, since the yearly directions gave such a strong indication of marriage, these monthly directions served to reinforce the major directions and to precipitate the anticipated event.

A striking instance of the value of monthly progressions occurs in the tragic case of the Lindbergh baby, who was kidnapped and murdered when only twenty months old. When events of such magnitude occur so soon after birth there is hardly time for any major directions to form which are not already close to exactitude in the radical chart. In cases of this nature the monthly directions are doubly valuable, both in confirming the testimony of the radical portents and in establishing the exact timing of the events which are forshadowed.

The monthly progressions in force in the horoscope of Charles A. Lindbergh, Jnr. at the time of his death were as follows—:

M.C. p. ⚻ ♄ r.   ☉ p. ☌ M.C., ♀ r.   ☿ p. □ ♅ p.
M.C. p. □ ☽ r.   ☉ con. ⚻ ♄ con.   ♀ p. □ ♂ p.
(applying)   (applying)
M.C. con. ☌ ☉ r.   ♀ con. ☍ ♄ con.
M.C. con. ✶ ♆ r.
Asc. con. □ ☉ r.   8th cusp p. □ ♆ r.

Here are all the ingredients of tragedy. The menacing square between the radical Uranus and Pluto, lying across the angles of the birth chart, is inflamed by the conjunction of the progressed Sun with Pluto and by the square between the progressed Mercury and the progressed Uranus, Mercury being placed in the Eighth House at birth. In the nativity, Mars and the Moon, the dispositors of Uranus and Pluto, form an ominous conjunction on the cusp of the Eighth House. The progressed Midheaven is applying to the square of the radical Moon, while the progressed Mars is receiving the application of the progressed Venus, the ruler of the chart and of the Eighth House, by square aspect. The Sun, as the dispositor of Venus, is especially important in this chart and its radical opposition to Saturn is given fresh emphasis by the quincunx between the two bodies by converse direction. The progressed Midheaven is in quincunx to the radical Saturn, and the converse Venus is in opposition to the converse Saturn. The only technically good aspect, the sextile between the converse Midheaven and the radical Neptune, is vitiated by the fact that Neptune is in detriment and in sesquiquadrate to the radical Uranus. To make matters worse, the progressed eighth cusp is in square to Neptune.

The monthly directions in Colonel Lindbergh's horoscope at the time of the tragedy were these:—

M.C. p. □ ♀ r.   ☉ r. ☌ ☿ p.   ♄ p. ⚻ ♆ p.
M.C. p. □ ♅ con.   ☉ r. △ ♂ p.   ♀ p. ☌ ♃ p. ✶ ☽ r.
M.C. con. ⚻ ♂ r.   ☉ con. ✶ ♅ r.   ☿ p. △ ♀ r.
M.C. con. □ ♆ con.   (separating)   ♀ con. ⚻ ♆ r.
M.C. con. (yearly) ☍ ☉ con.   ♂ r. △ ♆ con.
Asc. p. ⚻ ♆ p.   ☿ con. ☌ ♀ r.
Asc. con. □ ♂ con.

8th cusp p. ☌ ♆ p. ⚻ ♄ p.
8th cusp con. ☍ ♄ con.

Among the ominous group of angular directions operative at this time, the most threatening aspect is the square between the progressed monthly Midheaven and the radical Pluto. The converse monthly Uranus forms a T-square with these two points. This configuration is rendered even more critical on account of the fact that Uranus in the nativity is in almost exact square to the Midheaven and, in the yearly series of directions, is squared by the progressed Mars which has moved to the opposition of the radical Midheaven. Mars is the ruler of the radical Fifth House and Uranus is its dispositor. Two of the monthly progressions involve afflictions from Mars to the angles, and two involve similar afflictions from Neptune. Mars is in trine to Neptune in the nativity. The monthly solar aspects are technically favourable but the sextile between the converse monthly Sun and the radical Uranus, which is the more important because the Sun is simultaneously in opposition to the converse yearly Midheaven, only serves to inflame the square in the yearly series between the yearly progressed Mars and the radical Uranus. It should also be noted that Uranus in the nativity receives aspects from the other four malefic planets, Mars, Saturn, Neptune and Pluto. There is also a trine between the progressed monthly Mars and the radical Sun, Mars falling on the radical Part of Fortune. Mars, however, is in detriment and is also applying to the trine of the radical Pluto.

Saturn and Neptune in the progressed monthly series have formed an exact quincunx and the progressed Eighth House cusp in the monthly chart has reached the conjunction of the progressed Neptune, while the converse Eighth House cusp is in opposition to the converse Saturn. Several of the remaining interplanetary aspects are technically favourable but they are of little avail against the general malefic trend of the angular monthly directions. To the effect of these favourable directions may possibly be traced the fact that it was not until some weeks after the kidnapping that it became certain that the Lindbergh baby had been murdered.

In this chapter the indications of the monthly series of progressions have been considered largely without reference to the major directions which were simultaneously in force. Further examples of monthly progressions are given in Chapter XIII, which deals with the method of correlating the monthly, weekly and daily series of progressions with the yearly series.

Chapter X

THE WEEKLY SERIES OF SECONDARY DIRECTIONS

It has been demonstrated in Chapters II and IX that it is feasible to equate the passage of a day before or after birth to a period of a year or a month in the life of the native. After the month the next shortest single unit of time is the week and it will be the purpose of this chapter to introduce yet another series of directions based on the diurnal time unit, the Weekly Series.

The seven-day week has long been a feature of our Western Calendar. The parallel of the seven Days of Creation in the first chapter of Genesis at once springs to mind, although the "day" of Genesis, of course, covers a huge period of time. Nevertheless, as above, so below, and the correspondence still holds good. It may be objected that the seven-day week was abandoned for a time by Soviet Russia and that the Hebrew and the Mahommedan Calendars differ in some respects from our own, nevertheless, the acceptance of the Gregorian Calendar over the greater part of the civilised world points strongly to its correspondence to true cosmic principles.

Students of astrology will scarcely need to be reminded that the seven days of the week are named after the seven planets known in ancient Chaldea. The planet ruling each period of twenty-four hours is also held to have particular rule over the first hour after sunrise on that day. Thus the Sun rules the sunrise hour on Sunday, the Moon on Monday, Mars on Tuesday, Mercury on Wednesday, Jupiter on Thursday, Venus on Friday and Saturn on Saturday. It will thus be seen that the week is a natural, self-contained unit of time which has been recognized from the very earliest beginnings of human history.

The potency of the Weekly Series of progressions must, in the very nature of things, be less than that of the Yearly Series and the Monthly Series but their influence is not by any means negligible. These progressions are particularly useful in determining the precise period of action of a direction forming in the Yearly Series. As will be shown in Chapter XIII, their maximum value is attained when they are correlated with the directions formed by the three other directional measures which make up the complete Secondary or Arabian System. Just as it is often possible to predict successfully by transits alone, so it will be found that accurate prognostication is possible by using only the day-for-a-week measure. The microcosm reflects the macrocosm, and the picture in miniature formed by the day-for-a-week progressions must accurately mirror the condition of the major progressions forming at the same time.

Just as, in the Yearly Series of progressions, the major planets, due to their slow motion, cast their influence over whole years at a time, so it will be found that the same slow movement of the major planets sets the stellar tempo for whole weeks at a time in the Weekly Series of progressions.

It is well known that important changes take place in the human body every seven years. This seven year rhythm has not hitherto been satisfactorily emphasized in any system of astrological progression, except approximately in the case of the progressed Moon in the Yearly Series, which completes its circuit of the Zodiac in just over twenty-seven days, moving ninety degrees in the process in approximately seven days, the equivalent of seven years of time. The Weekly Series of progressions, however, divides itself almost exactly into seven year periods for, at the end of every seven years in the life, the Sun will have made one complete circuit of the Zodiac when progressed at the rate of a day for a week. The return of the Sun to the same position that it held at birth causes the radical chart to be charged with a fresh impulse of power at this time. A brief study of the tables for the Weekly Series of progressions which will be found at the end of this volume (Appendix I, Table 3) will form a graphic illustration of the exactness and regularity of this seven-year rhythm.

As in the case of the Yearly and Monthly Series of progressions, the Weekly Series are measured both forwards and backwards from the date of birth. The two sets of directions should be carefully correlated with each other, and with the natal chart and the Yearly Series of directions. As before, the difference between the Sun's position on the day measuring to the week under review and the Sun's position at birth is either added or subtracted from the radical Midheaven degree according to whether progressed or converse directions are being calculated. The Ascendant corresponding to the new Midheaven thus obtained should then be extracted from the Tables of Houses for the appropriate latitude.

The following is an example of the calculation of Weekly Secondary Directions. It is required to ascertain the weekly directions in force in the horoscope of Ann Harding during the third week in October, 1926:—

Date of birth..7th August, 1902
Date for which directions are required..................21st October, 1926
Number of years, months and days after birth......24 years, 2 months, 14 days
$$= 8,841 \text{ days}$$
$$= 1,263 \text{ weeks}$$
1,263 days after birth.................................21st January, 1906
1,263 days before birth...............................20th February, 1899
    (A Table simplifying the calculation of directional days before and after birth in the Weekly Series of progressions is provided in Appendix I.)

Calculation of the Progressed Weekly Midheaven:—

Sun's position at noon on 21st January, 1906................... 0° ♒ 34′
Sun's position at noon on day of birth........................ 14° ♌ 02′

Difference .... 5 signs 16° 32′

Position of radical Midheaven...........................		27° ♍ 39′
*Add difference between Sun positions................ 5 signs	16°	32′

Position of Progressed Weekly Midheaven..................	14° ♓ 11′

By referring to the Tables of Houses for 29°N.47′ we find that the
Ascendant corresponding to this Midheaven is.................. 29° ♊ 41′

The Converse Weekly Midheaven is calculated as follows:—
Sun's position at noon on day of birth........................ 14° ♌ 02′
Sun's position at noon on 20th February, 1899.................. 1° ♓ 40′

Difference .... 5 signs 12° 22′

Position of radical Midheaven........................... 27° ♍ 39′
†Subtract difference between Sun positions.............5 signs 12° 22′

Position of Converse Weekly Midheaven.................... 15° ♈ 17′

By referring to the Tables of Houses for 29°N.47′ we find that the
Ascendant corresponding to this Midheaven is.................. 24° ♋ 55′

All that remains now is to tabulate the aspects formed between the various
radical, progressed and converse angles and planets in the same manner as for the
Yearly and Monthly Series of Secondary Directions. Particular attention should be
paid to any progressed or converse weekly planets aspecting the progressed or
converse yearly angles, or the radical Ascendant or Midheaven. Contacts between
the weekly planets and the angles of the monthly progressions are also important.

As explained in the previous chapter, there is little point in taking into account
the progressed lunar aspects in the minor measures, since the daily progressions will
form an accurate method of timing the moment when progressed aspects in the
yearly, monthly and weekly series are likely to discharge their effects.

These are the weekly directions in the case under consideration:—

M.C. r. △ ♃ p. (applying)	☉ con. ☌ ♄ p.
M.C. r. △ ♀ p. (applying)	☉ con. △ yearly ♆ con.
M.C. con. ☐ ♀ con. ☐ ♀ r.	♀ p. △ ♃ p. (applying) ☌ yearly ♄ con.
Asc. con. ☍ ♀ p.	♂ p. ☐ ♀ r.
	♂ con. ⚻ ♀ r.
Yearly Asc. con. ☍ ♃ p.	☿ p. ☍ ♂ r.
Yearly Asc. p. ☌ ♅ p.	♀ con. ☍ ♀ r.
	♄ con. ☍ ♆ con.

* In cases where the difference is in excess of six signs it will often be found more convenient to *subtract*
the complementary part of the Zodiac.
   † In cases where the difference is in excess of six signs it will often be found more convenient to *add* the
complementary part of the Zodiac.

These were the weekly directions in force at the time of Ann Harding's first marriage. We have already seen how this event was clearly shown by the yearly and monthly directions which measured to this period.

The most significant aspect is the grand trine which is forming between the progressed weekly Venus and Jupiter and the radical Midheaven. Jupiter, moreover, is in opposition to the converse yearly Ascendant and Venus is joined with the converse yearly Saturn, both these bodies being at the same time in opposition to the converse weekly Ascendant. The converse weekly Midheaven is forming a T-square with the radical Venus and the converse weekly Venus which is in opposition to its own place in the nativity. The progressed weekly Uranus is in conjunction with the progressed yearly Ascendant, a contact which is the more significant on account of the proximity of Uranus to the Ascendant in the nativity. The converse weekly Mars is almost stationary in quincunx to the radical Seventh House Pluto and the progressed weekly Mars is in square to the radical Pluto. Any Mars-Pluto aspect intensifies the male principle, particularly in relation to partnership, and is therefore an important contact in a woman's chart at the time of marriage.

Of the three other contacts not so far mentioned, two involve planets in the Seventh House in the domestic sign Cancer and the other is between the converse weekly Sun and the progressed weekly Saturn in Pisces, which are both in trine to the converse yearly Neptune, their dispositor.

Once again it is the progressions involving the angles, especially the progressed yearly angles, which set the stage for the event. Although the Venus-Jupiter direction is a degree from exactitude, it is probably the exact opposition of the converse weekly Ascendant with the progressed weekly Venus which is the determining factor in precipitating the event during the week in question.

The second example of weekly directions is taken from the progressions in the chart of Charles Lindbergh, Jnr. measuring to the fatal week in which he was kidnapped and met his death. The directions are as follows:—

M.C. p. ☍ ♅ r.	☉ con. □ ♄ p.	♅ p. □ ♂ ♃ p. (mid-point)
Asc. r. ☌ ♀ con.		♅ con. □ ♄ con.
		♀ con. □ ♇ r. ☍ ♅ r.
		□ ♇ con.

The key direction here is probably the arrival of the converse weekly Venus at the conjunction of the radical Ascendant. Such a contact considered on its own, without regard to the rest of the horoscope, would appear, technically, to bring great benefit, as Venus is in its own sign, Libra, and is the ruler of the Ascendant, In this nativity, however, such an interpretation is completely contradicted by the affliction of the rising degree by the square of the radical Pluto and the opposition of the radical Uranus. The square between these two planets is made the more serious by the fact that Saturn opposes Pluto, forming the third point of a T-square. Even were this not the case, the heavier afflictions formed in the yearly and monthly series of progressions would completely outweigh the testimony of a single favourable aspect in the weekly series.

As Venus is the ruler, both of the Ascendant and of the Eighth House, this direction is extremely critical, for the planet of harmony is in square to the converse weekly Pluto and is midway between an aspect of the radical Pluto and the radical Uranus. Uranus is the most active planet in these weekly progressions and one glance at the birth chart will suffice to show the menacing import of the planet in relation to this child's life. The progressed weekly Midheaven is in opposition to the radical Uranus, the converse weekly Uranus is in square to the converse weekly Saturn, and the progressed weekly Uranus is in square to the point bracketed by the progressed weekly Mars and Jupiter, a contact made still worse by the fact that Mars in the nativity is on the cusp of the Eighth House, in detriment and in semi-square to Jupiter. This train of adverse directions is completed by a square between the converse weekly Sun and the progressed weekly Saturn. The Sun is the dispositor of Venus in the radical chart, thereby increasing the importance of this direction.

The weekly directions in the chart of Colonel Charles Lindbergh at the time of the same tragic event were as follows:—

M.C. p. ⚹ ♂ con.	♇ con. ⚻ ♂ r.
M.C. con. □ ♇ r.	♅ con. □ ♂ r.
M.C. con. ☌ ☉ p.	♃ p. □ ♄ p. ☌ ♇ con.
Asc. con. ⚹ ♂ con.	♂ p. ☌ ♇ r.
	♃ con. □ ♆ r.
Yearly Asc. p. □ ♇ con.	♄ con. ⚻ ♆ r.
	♄ r. ⚻ ♇ p.
☉ con. ⚹ ☽ r. △ ♂ r.	♅ p. ☍ ♆ p.
☉ r. △ ♇ con.	♆ con. ☍ ☽ ♅ r. (mid-point)

This group of directions is remarkable for the number of interplanetary aspects formed, many of them between the major planets and all of them unfavourable. In addition, the converse weekly Mars, Saturn and Uranus are all in Scorpio, which places an extra emphasis on the directions involving Pluto. We have seen how, in the yearly progressions, Mars had reached the square of the radical Uranus and the opposition of the radical Midheaven, while in the monthly series the monthly progressed Midheaven was in square to the radical Pluto. In the weekly directions listed above, Mars and Pluto figure most prominently, the most important aspect being the conjunction between the progressed weekly Mars and the radical Pluto, which excites the square between the Midheaven and Pluto in the monthly series.

The technically favourable Solar aspects are vitiated by the fact that Mars and Pluto are the planets primarily involved. Not only are these planets the chief mischief-makers in the progressions, but in the nativity Mars is involved with Uranus and Neptune, while Pluto is in opposition to Uranus, which is in square to the Midheaven.

The radical trine between the Sun and Pluto is now close to exactitude in the weekly progressions. This is a critical contact as the Sun at birth is in detriment and the progressed weekly Saturn, which is squared by the progressed weekly Jupiter, is in conjunction with the converse weekly Pluto.

The quincunx between the progressed weekly Pluto and the radical Saturn is another most critical direction, for Saturn is in square to the radical Fifth House cusp. The importance of the Martian directions is stressed by the contacts between the converse weekly Mars and the progressed weekly Midheaven and converse weekly Ascendant, together with aspect between the converse weekly Sun and the radical Mars. Although these three contacts are technically favourable, they merely serve to stimulate the battery of afflictions in force and do not in any way mitigate the effect of the adverse interplanetary contacts involving Mars, the ruler of the radical Fifth House.

The squares between the radical Venus and the converse weekly Midheaven, and between the converse weekly Venus and the progressed yearly Ascendant are similarly lacking in power to relieve the tension, as Venus in the birth chart is in Pisces, in square to the Ascendant and in conjunction with Mars, although simultaneously in trine and sextile to Neptune and the Moon respectively. Neptune, the dispositor of Venus, is heavily handicapped by its progressed weekly aspects with Jupiter, Saturn and Uranus. The prominence of Venus and the few technically favourable aspects may account for the fact that at the time of the kidnapping there was still hope for the baby's safety.

Further examples of weekly progressions will be found in Chapter XIII, in which the method of correlating the yearly, monthly, weekly and daily series of progressions is set forth.

Chapter XI

THE DAILY SERIES OF SECONDARY DIRECTIONS

THE final link in the chain of predictive methods which make up the new comprehensive system of Secondary Directing is the Daily Series of Progressions. We have already shown, both in theory and in practice, that it is valid to equate the passage of each True Solar Day before and after birth to a specific year, month or week in the life. In the Daily Series, the day is equated with itself, so that the current progressed daily directions for every person alive to-day measure to the immediate present. In this measure will at once be recognized the system of Transits, which has long been an accepted feature of astrological technique. The writer believes this to be the first time, however, that the idea has been put forward that Transits are an integral part of the system of Secondary Directions. Readers are probably also aware of the progressed Daily Horoscope, which has enjoyed a certain amount of popularity among astrologers. Just as in the Yearly Series of directions the progressions after birth furnish less than half of the total picture, so in the Daily Series of directions the progressed Daily Horoscope and Transits are only a part of the system. As in the Yearly, Monthly and Weekly Series, the same number of days must be measured off before birth as after birth in order to make an accurate estimate of all the influences in force. Once again, the number of degrees moved by the Midheaven is made to correspond exactly with the amount of the Sun's motion forwards and backwards through the Zodiac between the day of birth and the directional day.

The particular importance of the converse daily directions should at once become apparent if we consider, as an example, a cross-country race in which fifty competitors are taking part. The planets' positions in the heavens at the moment when the race is started are alike not only for all the competitors and all the spectators but, indeed, for the whole of humanity. These planetary influences which hold sway in the immediate present represent the common experiences of all mankind which arise from their simultaneous existence on this planet. The contacts which these present positions (transits) make with the birth charts of each one of us show the impact that these common experiences make on each individually. Each brings with him his own outlook, his own bundle of reactions, his own strengths and weaknesses, which are represented not only by his birth horoscope but by the development of that horoscope in terms of the various series of progressions, of which the Daily Series represents the ultimate unfoldment. Since the progressed daily positions at any given moment of time are the same for the whole of humanity, it is only by means of the converse daily positions that a complete and personal equation can be established between the individual and that immediate present which is common to all of us.

Therefore, in order to determine which competitors are likely to be most successful in the race, it is the converse daily directions which we must consult, for through them alone can we obtain indications which are sufficiently divergent to allow us to form a considered judgment. A study of the interplay between the converse daily directions and the native's radical chart and between the same converse directions and the progressed daily directions enables us to bring the daily events of the life into correct focus and to select from any given group of people, provided their birth data are accurately known, those who are most likely to meet with success or failure on a particular day.

A planet in the daily horoscope will make its influence most strongly felt when it is in strong aspect with a planet in the natal chart and at the same time in conjunction with or in opposition to the Midheaven or Ascendant of the daily chart. If it does not fall upon the angles of the daily horoscope its influence will be less striking and will be found to indicate minor events of the nature of the house of the radical chart and the sign through which it is passing. Aspects between the slower moving planets in the Daily Series and radical planets and angles will often remain within orbs for some weeks at a time and either the radical or the progressed planet will eventually become angular in the daily horoscope. At such a time the aspect will reach its maximum influence and its effects will make themselves felt most noticeably. The day on which a slow-moving planet forms an exact aspect with a radical planet or angle is also significant, but not quite to the same extent. A faster moving planet which simultaneously aspects both the radical and the daily progressed planet will often stimulate the contact to action. Of the faster-moving planets, Mars often produces the most noticeable effects when blending its rays in this manner with other planets in the daily series.

A combination of two or more of the heavier daily planets in aspect with radical or yearly progressed planets and angles is likely to indicate a significant event. The slower the rate of motion of the planets concerned the more important the event is likely to be. In this respect it should be noted that sometimes Mars, Venus and Mercury temporarily become slow-moving planets owing to their periods of retrograde motion, when they remain in the same two or three degrees of the Zodiac for several days or more at a time.

The progressed and converse angles of the daily horoscope make one complete circuit of the Zodiac in the course of the year. This means that on the same day in every year the angles will pass over the same radical planets. The effects of these annual contacts must therefore be of very little significance when considered alone, otherwise the pattern of events would tend to be repeated to a certain extent year after year. It is the actual places of the planets in the heavens which give significance to the progressed daily horoscope. This significance is increased when the daily planets are conjoined with the angles of the daily horoscope and at the same time in major aspect with the radical planets and angles.

The Daily Horoscope should be calculated for the place where the native happens to be on the day in question. Thus the Midheaven degree of the chart on that day will be the same wherever he may be but the Ascendant will vary according to the latitude of the place.

The following is an example of the calculation of Daily Secondary Progressions. It is required to ascertain the daily directions in force in the horoscope of Ann Harding for the 21st October, 1926, when she married for the first time:—

Date of birth..7th August, 1902
Date for which directions are required.................21st October, 1926
Number of years and days after birth......................24 years 75 days
24 years 75 days before birth.............................23rd May, 1878

(A table simplifying the calculation of directional days before birth in the Daily Series of progressions is provided in Appendix I.)

Calculation of Progressed Daily Midheaven:—
    Sun's position at noon on 21st October, 1926................... 27° ♎ 20′
    Sun's position at noon on day of birth....................... 14° ♌ 02′

    Difference .... 2 signs   13°   18′

    Position of radical Midheaven.............................. 27° ♍ 39′
    *Add difference between Sun positions.................. 2 signs   13°   18′

    Position of Progressed Daily Midheaven..................... 10° ♐ 57′

    By referring to the Tables of Houses for 40° N. 43′ we find that the
    Ascendant corresponding to this Midheaven is.................. 25° ♒ 42′

The Converse Daily Midheaven is calculated as follows:—
    Sun's position at noon on day of birth...................... 14° ♌ 02′
    Sun's position at noon on 23rd May, 1878...................... 2° ♊ 11′

    Difference .... 2 signs   11°   51′

    Position of radical Midheaven.............................. 27° ♍ 39′
    *Subtract difference between Sun positions............. 2 signs   11°   51′

    Position of Converse Daily Midheaven....................... 15° ♋ 48′

    By referring to the Tables of Houses for 40° N. 43′ we find that the
    Ascendant corresponding to this Midheaven is ....13° ♎ 37′

All that now remains is to tabulate the aspects formed between the various radical, progressed and converse angles and planets in the same manner as for the Yearly, Monthly and Weekly Series of Secondary Directions. Particular attention should be paid to any aspects formed between progressed or converse daily planets

* In cases where the difference is in excess of six signs, it will often be found more convenient to *subtract* the complementary part of the Zodiac instead of adding the larger part, and conversely, when a subtraction has to be made, it will often be easier to *add* the complementary part.

and the progressed or converse yearly angles, or the radical Ascendant or Midheaven. Contacts between the daily planets and the angles of the monthly and weekly progressions are also important, but to a lesser degree.

We have already observed, in connection with the slower measures, that it is unnecessary to pay particular attention to any lunar aspects formed, on account of the Moon's speedy progress through the Zodiac. It will be appreciated, therefore, that there is even less need to take into account aspects formed by the progressed daily Moon, unless it should be a New or a Full Moon, or unless it should occult a planet, and at the same time fall on a sensitive point in the nativity. The importance of Eclipses, New Moons and Full Moons is discussed in the next chapter.

In the case under consideration, the following are the daily directions:—

M.C. con. ☌ ♀ r. ☌ ♇ p.   ☉ con. ⊻ ♆ r.
M.C. p. ✶ ♃ r. (applying)   ☉ p. ✶ ♆ p.
M.C. p. △ ☿ r.
M.C. r. ⊻ ☉ p.   ☽ r. △ ♃ con.
Asc. p. △ ☉ p. ☍ ♆ p.   ☿ con. ✶ ♂ r. ☐ ♃ r.
Asc. con. ✶ ☉ r.   ☿ p. ☐ ♃ p.
Asc. con. △ ♃ r. (separating)   ♀ p. △ ☿ r.
Asc. con. ☐ ♂ r. (separating)   ♀ con. ✶ ♃ p. △ ♅ r.
Asc. r. ⊼ ♂ p.   ♂ con. ☌ ♂ r. (applying)
                                   ♅ p. ⊼ ♆ p.
                                   ♅ con. ☐ ♀ con. ☐ ♄ p.

Here we find an imposing array of aspects, the most impressive of which is the conjunction of the converse daily Midheaven with the radical Venus and the progressed daily Pluto. The progressed daily Venus is in trine to the radical Pluto, while the converse daily Venus is in trine to the radical Uranus and in sextile to the progressed daily Jupiter, which is midway between the Venus-Uranus trine. In the birth chart the Pluto-Uranus opposition falls across the cusps of the First and Seventh Houses and is therefore of primary importance in relation to the question of marriage.

The progressed daily Sun in Libra is in semi-sextile to the radical Midheaven, in sextile to the progressed daily Neptune, which was in the Seventh House at birth, and in trine to the progressed daily Ascendant, as in the nativity. The daily Ascendant and Neptune are in opposition, while the converse daily Sun is in semi-sextile to the radical Neptune.

The converse daily Ascendant picks up the trine between the radical Sun and Jupiter, applying to the sextile of the first-named body and separating from the trine of the second.

Mars, signifying the male principle, and having a relationship with the passional nature, is nearly always active in a woman's horoscope at the time of marriage. Here we find the progressed daily Mars in quincunx to the radical Ascendant, and the converse daily Ascendant separating from the square of the radical Mars, while the converse daily Mars is applying to the conjunction of its radical place. The converse daily Mercury, the ruler of the Seventh House, is in sextile to the radical Mars.

A contact between the rulers of the First and Seventh Houses is to be expected at the time of marriage. Here, the converse daily Mercury is in square to the radical Jupiter, and the progressed daily Mercury and Jupiter are also in square to each other. The progressed daily Midheaven is in trine to the radical Mercury.

Of the remaining aspects the trine between the converse daily Jupiter and the radical Moon in Libra is most helpful, but the afflictions between the progressed daily Uranus and Neptune, and between the converse daily Uranus and Pluto, which form a T-square with the progressed daily Saturn, no doubt have a bearing upon the fact that the marriage was not a lasting one.

The Lindbergh baby was kidnapped and murdered on 1st March, 1932, when the following daily progressions had formed in his horoscope:—

M.C. p. ⊼ ♆ con. □ ☉ r.	☉ con. □ ♀ r.
M.C. con. ☌ ☿ con. ☍ ♃ con.	☉ r. ⚹ ♆ con.
Asc. r. ☍ ♅ p.	☉ p. ⚹ ☽ r.
Asc. p. ☌ ♀ r. □ ☉ con.	
	☿ p. ⚹ ♂ r.
Yearly M.C. p. ☌ ♀ p. □ ♀ p.	☿ con. ⚹ ♄ r.
	☿ p. □ ♄ con.
	♀ p. □ ♀ p.
	♂ r. ⊼ ♄ con.

Once again the planet Pluto plays a prominent part in the daily directions. The importance of this planet in all progressions in the horoscopes of Ann Harding and the Lindbergh baby is emphasized by its angular position in both nativities. In the horoscope now under consideration the radical Pluto is squared by Uranus. These two planets are placed respectively on the Midheaven and on the Descendant, and their dispositors, the Moon and Mars, are in threatening conjunction on the cusp of the Eighth House. Here, in the radical chart, are all the ingredients of tragedy. The atmosphere of ill-omen, already established by the major progressions for the year, becomes charged with the most deadly menace when considered in the light of the daily aspects listed above.

The progressed daily Ascendant has reached the conjunction of the radical Pluto and the converse daily Sun has reached the square of the same planet. The progressed daily Venus, the ruler of the natal Ascendant, is in square to the progressed daily Pluto, which is also in conjunction with the progressed yearly Midheaven. The progressed daily Uranus reached the exact opposition of the radical Ascendant on the previous day.

The radical Moon and Mars on the cusp of the Eighth House are stimulated by sextiles from the progressed daily Sun and Mercury respectively. The converse daily Neptune is very close to the exact sextile of the radical Sun, a contact which is made less favourable by the position of Neptune in Virgo, the sign of its fall. The progressed daily Midheaven picks up this Sun-Neptune contact, forming a square with the Sun, and a quincunx with Neptune.

A second quincunx occurs between the converse daily Saturn and the radical Mars. The trine between the two bodies in the nativity is spoilt by Mars being in debility. The radical quincunx between Mercury and Saturn is re-emphasized by a double contact between the two planets in the daily progressions, the converse daily Mercury being in sextile to the radical Saturn, and the progressed daily Mercury in square to the converse daily Saturn. The converse daily Midheaven, separating from the opposition of the converse daily Jupiter and applying to the conjunction of the converse daily Mercury, is equally poised between the two. The opposition occurs from Taurus to Scorpio and appears to be an indication of the huge publicity accorded to the tragedy.

The progressions operative in Colonel Lindbergh's horoscope on the same day were these:—

M.C. p. △ ☉ r. △ ♀ r.   ☽ r. ⊼ ♃ con.
M.C. con. ☍ ♂ r. (separating)   ♀ p. □ ♄ r. ♂ ♆ con. □ ♀ p.
Asc. r. □ ♂ p. (separating)   ♀ p., ♆ con. ♂ 5th cusp r.
Asc. p. ♂ ☽ ♅ r. (mid-point)   ♀ r. ⊻ ♄ p.
Asc. con. □ ☉ r. □ ♃ p. △ ☿ p.   ♀ con. □ ♂ p.
Asc. r. ⊻ ☿ con.   ♂ con. □ ♀ con.
                                   ♃ r. ☍ ♅ con.
☉ r. ☍ ♃ p.   ♄ r. ☍ ♀ p.
☉ r. ⊻ ☿ p.
☉ con. △ ♀ con.

The key aspects here are the grand trine between the progressed daily Midheaven and the radical Sun and Pluto, and the formidable T-square which has built up on the cusp of the radical Fifth House. The planets involved in this T-square are the progressed daily Venus, the converse daily Neptune, the progressed daily Pluto and the radical Saturn, the two first-named forming the fulcrum of the affliction exactly on the menaced cusp.

The importance of the trine between the radical Sun and Pluto is underlined by the fact that both bodies are in close trine to the Part of Fortune. From the material standpoint this contact is vitiated by the Sun being in Aquarius, the sign of its fall. As Aquarius is the opposite sign to Leo, the sign of children, fresh emphasis is thus placed upon the condition of the radical fifth cusp, especially as Pluto and Saturn, the co-dispositor of the Sun, are concerned in the malevolent configuration involving that cusp. The radical Sun-Pluto trine is repeated by the converse daily Sun and Pluto, a phenomenon which at once serves to underline the stark significance of this fateful day.

In the light of these testimonies the remaining daily directions can only serve as corroborative evidence of the fatal event. The progressed daily Ascendant is bracketed by the radical Moon-Uranus conjunction, threatening an upheaval in the domestic life. The converse daily Midheaven has just separated from the opposition of the radical Mars in Aquarius, while the progressed daily Mars in Pisces, the sign of sorrows, is just separating from the square of the radical Ascendant. The converse daily Ascendant in Scorpio picks up the opposition between the radical Sun in Aquarius and the progressed daily Jupiter in Leo.

Mercury, which squares the Ascendant at birth from the sign Pisces and disposes of both Neptune and Pluto, has progressed to the semi-sextile of the radical Sun and has formed a similar aspect with the radical Ascendant by converse motion. Of the remaining group of interplanetary aspects, only one, the semi-sextile between the progressed daily Saturn and the radical Venus, is technically favourable, but any beneficial influence is completely undermined by the overwhelming weight of afflictions centred on the progressed Venus and the radical Saturn. The contact is made the more critical by the radical Saturn being in the Second House, which, by reason of its opposition to the Eighth House, is connected with death. The squares between Venus and Mars and between Pluto and Mars weight the scales still more heavily, especially as Mars is the ruler of the Fifth House and is at the same time in square to Uranus in the yearly progressions, and in opposition to the radical Midheaven from Pisces, the sign of sorrows.

We have seen how the daily progressions of two of the members of the Lindbergh family indicated that 1st March, 1932, was to be a most fateful day in their lives. Similar configurations also occurred in the daily progressions of Anne Morrow Lindbergh's horoscope. Confronted with such a coincidence of threatening aspects in the horoscopes of three closely related people, an astrologer could scarcely avoid having grave misgivings lest some family catastrophe should take place on that particular day. These examples, therefore, show that the daily horoscope is of the very greatest significance and can play a vital part in determining critical days in the life.

The method of correlation of the daily series of progressions with the weekly, monthly and yearly series is set forth in Chapter XIII, which also contains further examples of daily progressions.

Chapter XII

THE DAILY SERIES OF SECONDARY DIRECTIONS FURTHER CONSIDERATIONS

THE methods of judging the daily series of directions described in the previous chapter were, in essence, the same as those used in judging the weekly, monthly and yearly series. There are, however, several additional factors which should be taken into account when considering the effects of the daily series of directions.

The first concerns the effect of lunations and eclipses falling on sensitive points of the radical or progressed horoscope. When the New or Full Moon is in strong close aspect to a planet or an angle of the birth chart, it is apt to excite events of the nature of the planet or the signs concerned. When such a configuration of the luminaries is in close aspect to a progressed planet or angle, which is itself forming an aspect with another planet or angle of the radical or progressed horoscope, it is likely to precipitate events of the nature of the direction which it stimulates. An orb of three degrees may be allowed when computing these lunation aspects.

New and Full Moons will operate most strongly when they stimulate the yearly progressions. They will also excite, in a similar way, directions in the monthly, weekly and daily series, although to a lesser degree. The results of these contacts of the luminaries will nearly always make themselves felt within a week or fortnight of the date on which they occur. Occasionally they will act to precipitate events a few days before the lunation actually falls due.

The following illustrations of the effects of New and Full Moons falling on sensitive places in the radical and progressed chart are taken from the example horoscopes on pages 147–149, and will form a useful basis for study:—

Anne Morrow Lindbergh.
    Son born, 22nd June, 1930.
        Full Moon—11th June. (20 ♐) ☍ ♃ ♀ r.
        New Moon—26th June. (4 ♋) ☌ ☉ ♂ r. (mid-point).
    Equivalent date before birth, 21st June, 1882.
        Full Moon—1st July. (9 ♑) ☍ ♆ ☽ ♂ r.
        New Moon—15th June. (24 ♊) ☌ ♃ ♀ r.
            Yearly directions stimulated:—
            M.C. p. ⊻ ♀ r.
                ♂ r. ⊻ ☉ con.
                ☉ r. ✳ ♀ p.

Daughter born, 2nd October, 1940.
    Full Moon—16th September. (23 ♓) □ ♃ ♀ r.
Equivalent date before birth, 11th March, 1882.

Full Moon—24th March.   (4♎)   ✶ ♀ r. □ ☉ ♂ r. ♋
New Moon—9th March.   (19♓) □ ♃ ♀ r. ☌ ♄ r.
  Yearly directions stimulated:—
      ☉ p. ☌ ♀ r.
      ♀ con. ☌ ♃ r.
(Note that the Jupiter-Pluto conjunction is stimulated at the birth of both children!)

Colonel Charles Lindbergh.

Became a Flying Cadet in Air Service of War Department, 19th March, 1924.
  New Moon—5th March.   (15♓) □ ♀ r.
      (♅ on 5th March in 17♓.)
Equivalent date before birth, 21st December, 1879.
  New Moon—13th December. (21♐) ☌ ♅ r.
      Yearly directions stimulated:—
          Asc. con. ⊼ ♀ r.
          Asc. p. ☌ ♅ con.

Trans-Atlantic Flight, 20th May, 1927.
  Full Moon—16th May.   (25♏) □ ♂ r. 3.
      (♆ on 16th May in 24♌, close to converse Midheaven.)
Equivalent date before birth, 21st October, 1876.
  New Moon—17th October.   (25♎) ✶ ☽ r. △ ♂ r.
      Yearly direction stimulated:—
          M.C. con. △ ☽ r.

Daughter born, 2nd October, 1940.
  Full Moon—16th September. (23♓) □ ☽♅ r.
Equivalent date before birth, 7th June, 1863.
  New Moon—16th June.   (25♊) ☍ ☽ r. △ ♂ ♒ r.
      Yearly directions stimulated:—
          ☉ p. (23♓) □ ☽♅ r. (mid-point).
          ♂ p. □ ☽ r.
          ☿ p. ✶ ☽ r. ☌ ♂ r.

Charles Lindbergh, Jnr.

Kidnapped, 1st March, 1932.
  New Moon—7th March.   (16♓) △ ♀ r.
      (Radical ♀ □ ♅ on angles of birth chart.)
Equivalent date before birth, 12th October, 1928.
  New Moon—13th October.   (20♎) □ ♀, M.C. r.

Ann Harding.

Lengthy visit to London, 10th February, 1937.
  New Moon—11th February. (22♒) ☌ 3rd cusp r.
      (The converse Midheaven was in 22♌.)

Equivalent date before birth, 31st January, 1868.
Full Moon—8th February. (19♌) ✶ ♀ ♊ r. △ ♅ r.
Yearly directions stimulated:—
☉ p. □ ♅ r.
♂ con. ☍ ♅ r. ☌ ♀ r.

Eclipses of the Sun and Moon stimulating directions or close radical aspects in the natal chart act with greatly increased intensity and their effect is spread over a wider span of time. Although, in some cases, the immediate results of an eclipse will be readily apparent, in others the effects may not make themselves felt until some months have passed. The average length of time elapsing before an eclipse takes effect appears to be five or six months but this period may be extended, in isolated cases, to as much as twelve months. Occasionally, the effects of an eclipse will be observed a few days before the phenomenon actually falls due. This margin of timing can be compared to the orb of four or five degrees before the cusp of each house in the horoscope, within which planets exert their major influence in terms of the house that they have just left by axial rotation. A study of the monthly, weekly and daily series of directions in force will provide the best clues as to when the eclipse is likely to operate most strongly. Two or three eclipses in succession strongly aspecting the same point are likely to produce the most marked effects. These effects are by no means always adverse, as tradition would have us believe, for they may equally stimulate favourable or unfavourable progressions or radical aspects.

Lunations and eclipses falling on sensitive points of the horoscope are nothing more than a double transit of the Sun and Moon. The pull exerted by these bodies is amply demonstrated in the realm of physical phenomena by the effect which they have on the tides. When the Sun and Moon are in conjunction or opposition their double pull causes the tide to rise higher than at other times. Their influence is similarly potent when applied to the sea of human experience and its individual expression in terms of each natal horoscope.

The following illustrations of the effects of Eclipses of the Sun and Moon falling on sensitive places in the radical and progressed chart are taken from the example horoscopes on pages 147–149, and will form a useful basis for study:—

Adolf Hitler.
Bavaria Putsch, 9th November, 1923.
Lunar Eclipse—26th August. (2♓) □ ♀ ♆ r. (mid-point).
Equivalent date before birth, 1st October, 1854.
Solar Eclipse—9th November. (17♏) □ ♄ r. ☍ ♂♀ r.
Yearly directions stimulated:—
☉ p. ☌ ♆ ♀ r. (mid-point).
12th cusp con. □♆ ♀ r. (mid-point).

Fuehrer of Germany, 30th January, 1933.
Solar Eclipse—31st August, 1932. (8♍) △ ♃ r.
Equivalent date before birth, 10th July, 1845.

Solar Eclipse—30th October. (7♏) ✶ ♃ r. ☍ ☉ ♂ r. (mid-point).
Yearly directions stimulated:—

  ♀ p. △ ♃ p.
  ♀ con. △ ♃ con.

Anne Morrow Lindbergh.

Son kidnapped, 1st March, 1932.
  Solar Eclipse—12th September, 1931. (18♍) ☍ ♄ r. □ ♃♀ r.
  (mid-point).

  Lunar Eclipse—26th September, 1931. (3 ♈) □ ☉ ♂ r. (mid-point)
  △ ♀ r.

  Solar Eclipse—7th March. (17♓) ☌ ♄ r. □ ♃♀ r.

Equivalent date before birth, 11th October, 1880.
  Lunar Eclipse—16th December, 1880. (25♊) ☌ ♀ r. □ Asc. r.
  Solar Eclipse—31st December, 1880. (10♑) ☍ ♆ ☽ ♂ r.
  Lunar Eclipse—12th June, 1881. (21♐) ☍ ♀ r.
    (Converse Mars in 20♊.)
    Yearly directions stimulated:—
      M.C. p. ☌ ♂ p.
      5th cusp con. ☍ ♆ ☽ ♂ r.
      ♃ con. □ ♄ con.

Colonel Charles Lindbergh.

Trans-Atlantic Flight, 20th May, 1926.
  Lunar Eclipse—15th June. (23♐) ☌ ☽ ♅ r. (mid-point).
Equivalent date before birth, 21st October, 1877.
  Solar Eclipse—2nd February, 1878. (13♒) ☌ ☉ r. 3.
    Yearly directions stimulated:—
      Asc. p. ☌ ♅ p.
      Asc. con. □ ☉ r.
      M.C. p. △ ☉ r. △ ♀ r.
      M.C. con. △ ☽ r.
      ☿ p. ✶ ♅ r.

Married, 27th May, 1929.
  Solar Eclipse—17th June, 1928. (26♊) ☍ ☽ r. △ ♂ r.
    (from Seventh House.)
  Lunar Eclipse—27th November, 1928. (5♊) ☌ 7th cusp r.
Equivalent date before birth, 14th October, 1874.
  Solar Eclipses—6th April, 1875. (16 ♈) ✶ ♀ r. 7.
  Lunar Eclipse—25th October, 1874. (2 ♉) ✶ ♀ r.
  Solar Eclipse—10th October, 1874. (17♎) △ ♀ r. 7.
    Yearly directions stimulated:—
      M.C. p. △ ♀ p. △ ♀ r.
      Asc. p. ☌ ☽ ♅ (mid-point).

Son kidnapped, 1st March, 1932.
  Solar Eclipse—12th September, 1931. (18♍) □ ♀ r. □ ♅ r.
  Solar Eclipse—11th October, 1931. (17♎) △ ☉ r. △ ♀ r.
  Solar Eclipse—7th March, 1932. (17♓) □ ♅ r. □ ♀ r.
Equivalent date before birth, 9th January, 1872.
  Solar Eclipse—6th June, 1872. (16♊) ☌ ♀ r.
  Lunar Eclipse—22nd May, 1872. (2♐) ☌ Asc. r. □ ♀ r.
      Yearly direction stimulated:—
        M.C. r. ☍ ♂ p.

Ann Harding.
  First marriage, 21st October, 1926.
    Solar Eclipse—9th July. (17♋) ☌ ♀ r.
  Equivalent date before birth, 23rd May, 1878.
    Lunar Eclipse—13th August. (20♒) △ ♀ r. 7.
    Solar Eclipse—29th July. (7♌) ⚹ ☽ ♎ r.
        Yearly direction stimulated:—
          ☉ p. ⚺ ☽ r.

  Second marriage, 17th January, 1937.
    Lunar Eclipse—8th January, 1936. (17♋) ☌ ♀ r.
    Lunar Eclipse—4th July, 1936. (12♑) ☍ ♀♂ r.
  Equivalent date before birth, 24th February, 1868.
    Solar Eclipse—23rd February, 1868. (4♓) △ ♆ r. 7.
        Yearly directions stimulated:—
          Asc. p. ☍ ♀ r.
          ♀ con. ⚺ ♆ r.

It is a significant commentary on the potency of eclipses that, for the eight events listed above, there are no fewer than twenty-eight eclipses, both before and after birth, falling on sensitive points of the horoscopes concerned. This average of three-and-a-half eclipses per event is by no means abnormal in cases where the events in question are of primary importance in the life.

Some text-books include delineations of the effects of planets passing through the houses of the radical chart. While it is true that the arrival of a planet by transit on the cusp of a house may have a noticeable effect, its mere presence by daily progression in that sector of the horoscope is of no special significance until it makes an aspect with another radical or progressed planet or angle, thus forming a direction in the daily series of progressions.

The slow motion of the major planets invests the aspects which they form with greater significance, especially so in the case of Pluto, which moves forward in the Zodiac about 1½ degrees per year, on the average. This rate is only slightly faster than that of the progressed yearly Sun and is sometimes slower than that of the progressed yearly Mercury or Venus. It is therefore reasonable to regard aspects formed by the daily motion of Pluto as having the potency of major secondary directions. Owing to the fluctuation of Pluto's movement in the Zodiac these aspects often form and reform in the course of a year. Each subsequent contact is likely to be felt more strongly than the previous one. This, by the way, holds good for most progressed aspects which are repeated several times owing to the retrograde motion of one of the planets concerned.

It is therefore recommended that special consideration should be given to aspects formed by the daily motion of Pluto to planets in the radical chart and to the progressed angles and planets in the yearly series of directions. This refers equally of course, to the aspects formed by the converse daily Pluto. For the interpretation of such aspects the reader is referred to the delineations of progressed aspects involving the radical Pluto, given in Chapters V, VI and VII.

The following illustrations of aspects formed by the daily progressed and converse Pluto are taken from the example horoscopes on pages 147-149 and will afford a useful basis for study:—

Charles Lindbergh, Jnr. M.C. r. ☌ ♇ p. Death.
Jay Gould. M.C. r. □ ♇ p. Death. M.C. r. ☌ ♇ con. President of Erie Railway. Daughter born.
Adolf Hitler. M.C. r. ☌ ♇ p. Munich Crisis. Invasion of Poland.
Madame Blavatsky. Asc. r. △ ♇ con. Marriage.
Henry Ford. Asc. r. ☍ ♇ p. Left home. Worked fourteen hours a day,
Ralph Waldo Emerson. Asc. r. ☍ ♇ p. House burnt down. Travelled to Egypt. Lost memory.
Albert Einstein. ☉ r. △ ♇ p. Took up residence in U.S.A.
Karl Marx. ☉ r. □ ♇ con. Tried for High Treason.
Adolf Hitler. ☉ r. ☌ ♇ con. Bavaria Putsch.
Karl Marx. ☽ r. ☌ ♇ p. Founded Working Men's International.
Ralph Waldo Emerson. ☽ r. △ ♇ p. Married. Appointed as Pastor.
Mary Baker Eddy. ☽ r. ☌ ♇ con. Second marriage.
Ralph Waldo Emerson. ☿ r. △ ♇ con. Travelled to Egypt. Memory began to fail.
Annie Besant. ☿ r. □ ♇ con. Toured with Krishnamurti.
Anne Morrow Lindbergh. ☿ r. ☌ ♇ p. Marriage. Record-breaking flight to the Orient.
Albert Einstein. ♀ r. ⚹ ♇ p. First marriage. ♀ r. ☌ ♇ con. Second marriage.
Karl Marx. ♀ r. ☌ ♇ p. Wife died.
Cecil Rhodes. ♂ r. □ ♇ con. Death.
Jay Gould. ♂ r. □ ♇ con. Death.
Annie Besant. ♂ r. ☌ ♇ p. Married. Birth of a son.
Madame Blavatsky. ♃ r. ☌ ♇ con. Founded Theosophical Society.
Henry Ford. ♃ r. △ ♇ p. Founded Ford Motor Company.
Cecil Rhodes. ♃ r. △ ♇ con. Went to brother's farm in Natal to build up health.
Henry Ford. ♄ r. △ ♇ p. Married. Built own house.
Jay Gould. ♄ r. △ ♇ con. Director of Union Pacific Railroad.
Karl Marx. ♄ r. □ ♇ con. Pleurisy. Death of wife.
Jay Gould. ♅ r. ☌ ♇ con. Made fraudulent stock sales. Forced to resign from company and make restitution.
Albert Einstein. ♅ r. △ ♇ con. Published *Restricted Theory of Relativity*.
   ♅ r. ⚹ ♇ p. Published *General Theory of Relativity*.
Madame Blavatsky. ♆ r. △ ♇ p. Founded Theosophical Society. ♆ r. ☌ ♇ con. *Secret Doctrine* published.
Karl Marx. ♆ r. △ ♇ p. Tried for High Treason.

Chapter XIII

THE COMPLETE SYSTEM OF SECONDARY DIRECTING

The Method of Correlation

In the preceding chapters it has been shown how the passage of each day before and after birth may be taken to represent a corresponding year, month, week or day in the life of the native. It has also been demonstrated how the aspects formed between the radical angles and planets and the progressed angles and planets on these directional days appear to coincide in a remarkable manner with events in the native's life. All that now remains to be done is to show how the directions in the Yearly, Monthly, Weekly and Daily Series may be co-ordinated and used with the maximum degree of efficiency.

It cannot be too strongly emphasized that it is the Yearly Series of Secondary Directions which establish the basic vibrations of the period under review. The Monthly, Weekly and Daily Series temporarily intensify or modify these vibrations, according to their own nature. The most powerful progressed aspects are those involving the radical and yearly progressed Midheaven and Ascendant. These, together with the yearly Solar aspects, must be given first consideration when assessing the likely events of the period.

The first operation, therefore, is to make a thorough survey of the Yearly Series of Directions in force in order to establish the type of event most likely to occur during the period. When a preliminary judgment has been formed, corroborative evidence may then be sought in the Monthly Series. Should such evidence not be forthcoming, it may then be necessary to modify the original forecast. If the indications of the Monthly Series appear to run contrary to those of the Yearly Series, the influence of the major series will not be overthrown thereby, but it may be diminished in intensity.

The importance of the angles of a horoscope derives from the fact that they are the "flash-points" of the chart through which are externalized the planetary vibrations. A planet attains its maximum influence in the life when it forms an exact aspect with an angle. It is this factor, above all others, which makes possible accurate prediction.

The progressed and converse Midheaven and Ascendant are even more sensitive than the radical angles, for whereas the latter may be compared to the foundation of a building, the former represents the superstructure built upon that foundation. In the event of unfavourable planetary weather arising, the superstructure is much less likely to withstand the impact than the foundations. The nativity, therefore, under normal circumstances, has the strength to survive much greater shocks than the progressed or converse horoscope. For this reason it is especially necessary to observe the aspects formed between the progressed and converse monthly, weekly and daily planets and the progressed and converse yearly angles. These aspects are of even greater significance if the yearly angles are already involved in an aspect with a radical planet or with a planet in the progressed or converse Yearly Series of directions.

When correlating the four series of progressions it is first necessary to note the zodiacal degrees occupied by the progressed and converse yearly Midheaven and Ascendant, as well as the natal positions of these major angles, and any radical or yearly planets which are in close aspect with them. Then the monthly progressions should be consulted in order to ascertain whether any planet in this series is within a degree of an exact aspect to any of the angular degrees already noted. Should any such aspects be formed, the days on which they occur will measure to the months when their effects are likely to be felt most strongly. If, in addition, the point aspected is also in contact with a radical or progressed planet, an event of major importance may then be anticipated. Such cross-aspects from the planets of the monthly series to the radical and progressed yearly angles will rarely be very numerous and it will accordingly be comparatively simple to determine the month or months when major directions are likely to operate with maximum effect.

Attention should next be paid to any aspects between the planets of the monthly series and planets which have reached an exact aspect in the yearly progressions. The month measuring to the day on which the aspect is completed will also be of considerable significance, producing events of the nature of the aspect formed in the yearly series of progressions. If, for example, the progressed yearly Mars reaches the square of the radical Jupiter fourteen days after birth and the progressed monthly Mercury reaches the square of the radical Jupiter one hundred and seventy days after birth—or fourteen years two months, if we take a day to represent a month—then the second month of the fifteenth year will be the time when the effects of the Mars square Jupiter yearly direction are most likely to be precipitated. But should Mars in the monthly series conjoin Jupiter in the birth chart five days after Mercury has completed the square to that planet, a further and probably more serious precipitation of the same major direction would then be likely to occur five months later.

The last special configurations to note in the monthly series are the aspects formed between the progressed monthly angles and the monthly planets. When a planet is in conjunction with an angle of the monthly figure but not in aspect with a radical or yearly progressed planet or angle, some minor event of the nature of that planet may be anticipated. If, on the other hand, the angular monthly planet touches up an aspect in the yearly series, most important events are likely to occur during that month.

As soon as it has been determined which months are likely to be of outstanding importance during the year, it is advisable to turn next to the corresponding weekly series of progressions in order to see whether similar conditions of crisis or climax during these months are also marked. Once again, it is the interplay between the planets of the weekly series and the radical angles and the progressed and converse yearly angles which are of paramount importance. In addition, great importance attaches to planets in the weekly series which touch up angular or interplanetary aspects formed in the yearly series, especially if a planet in the monthly series is also in aspect at the same time. Major results may also be anticipated if a planet of the weekly series falls on the angles of the progressed weekly figure, and completes, at the same time, a major aspect to the planets or angles of the birth chart or the progressed or converse angles or planets of the yearly series. It is also useful to keep a watch on the interplay between the various factors in the monthly and weekly charts. Aspects between the planets of the weekly series and the angles of the monthly figure are also highly significant. The principal attention, however, should be given to those weekly progressions which reinforce and underline the cross-aspects between the monthly and yearly series of progressions.

It is advisable when tabulating the directions formed by planets in the weekly series to check first of all those directions formed during the weeks which fall in the month or months previously selected as significant as a result of studying the directions in the monthly series. If, during these weeks, major aspects to directions in the yearly series are also formed, the likelihood of important events taking place at such times is accordingly strengthened. On the other hand, if no striking configurations occur, the probability of significant events taking place is diminished and it will accordingly become necessary either to seek fresh evidence or to weigh more carefully the evidence already obtained.

Events of lesser importance will be indicated by aspects formed between the various progressed planets of the weekly series.

If it is desired to estimate the particular day on which a direction will be likely to operate with maximum effect, it will be necessary to consult the daily series of progressions. In most cases the monthly and weekly series will already have indicated that a particular month or week is likely to be of special importance. It is then a comparatively simple matter to pick out the daily directions forming during the period which are most likely to bring matters to a head.

Planets of the daily series falling on the angles of the radical chart or on the progressed or converse yearly angles will produce the most important effects. Next in order of significance are aspects between planets of the daily series and progressed planets of the yearly series. A planet in the daily series arriving at an angle of the daily horoscope will produce some significant event on that day, but the event will be comparatively trivial in its effect unless the daily planet is at the same time in aspect with the planets or angles in the major progressions. Similarly, interplanetary aspects in the daily series are of little importance unless they are also in contact with planets or angles of the major progressions.

It will not always be necessary to follow the procedure outlined above in all its various stages. Once the year and the month have been determined by reference to the yearly and monthly series it is often possible to narrow down the period in which the direction will operate by direct reference to the daily series. Jupiter, Saturn, Uranus, Neptune and Pluto will, in the natural order of things, tend to remain in aspect with significant points in the progressed yearly horoscope for days and sometimes weeks at a time. The day on which their influence is likely to reach its peak is the day when they coincide with angles of the daily figure. The Sun, Mars, Venus and Mercury, however, speedily form and break off contacts with these significant points in the progressed yearly horoscope, and the day on which these contacts become exact will be the day on which events of the greatest significance are likely to happen, according to the nature of the planets involved.

It may sometimes be more convenient to go directly from the yearly series to the weekly series, omitting the monthly series of progressions, while occasionally it will be possible to obtain satisfactory results by jumping straight from the yearly progressions to the daily progressions. As readers will by now be aware, daily progressions consist of something more than the "transit" system which many astrologers use, since the most important features of the daily series are the converse directions and the progressed and converse angles of the daily chart.

A convenient summary of the principles involved in the correlation of the various series of progressions may be made as follows:—

(1) The Yearly Series of Directions indicates the dominant emphasis for the period under review. Directions involving the radical, progressed and converse angles exert the greatest influence.

(2) Events denoted by these angular directions in the Yearly Series are most likely to be precipitated when the radical, progressed or converse angle involved in the direction receives an aspect from a planet in one of minor series, whether monthly, weekly or daily. These contacts are of primary importance and indicate those months, weeks or days which are likely to be of the greatest significance, according to the measure used.

(3) Similarly, interplanetary directions in the Yearly Series are most likely to be stimulated to action when a planet in one of the minor series forms an exact aspect with the planets in the Yearly Series which are involved in the major direction. These contacts, also, will indicate significant months, weeks or days according to the measure used.

(4) Planets in the minor series arriving on an angle indicate a time of potential importance. Should a planet so placed not be in aspect with any significant point in the birth chart or with any major progressed planet or angle, its importance is much diminished.

(5) Interplanetary aspects in the minor series are not likely to produce effects of great importance unless contacts are formed at the same time with planets involved in major progressions.

It may appear that the foregoing procedure is a little complicated, but the student will soon gain proficiency in applying the various measures and will speedily learn to discriminate between that material which is of prime importance and that which is relatively insignificant.

For the sake of completeness, examples of the calculation of lunar progressions were given in Chapter II. It is not recommended, however, that progressed lunar aspects should be used in the new complete system of Secondary Directing, since the refinement of timing which was their primary function may now be more efficiently accomplished by using the monthly, weekly and daily series of progressions.

A problem arises in connection with this system of directing which readers may like to consider. It will be remembered that the daily horoscope should be erected for the actual place where the native is on the day in question. It would appear logical to make a similar adjustment in the yearly, monthly and weekly directions in those cases where the native moved an appreciable distance away from his birthplace shortly after birth. If, for instance, he was taken to live in a completely new locality only sixty days after he was born, it seems reasonable to suggest that the progressed horoscopes for his sixty-first year, sixty-first month and sixty-first week should properly be calculated for the new place of residence. As such cases are comparatively rare it has not yet been possible to arrive at a definite conclusion on this matter.

The following illustrations are taken from the example horoscopes on pages 147–149 and are set out in tabular form, thus providing a graphic demonstration of the manner in which the various series of directions act upon each other. These tables only include those minor directions which are directly linked by aspect with the major directions and radical positions and are not necessarily an exhaustive catalogue of all the monthly, weekly and daily directions operating at the time.

COLONEL CHARLES LINDBERGH
Child kidnapped, 1st March, 1932.

Series	*Directional Day*	1	2	3	4	5
Radical, Progressed and Converse Angles (Yearly)	Progressed 6th Mar., 1902.	M.C. r. 20½ ♍ M.C. p. 20½ ♎ Cusp 5r. 21 ♈		Asc. r. 3♐		
Radical, Progressed and Converse Planets (Yearly)	Converse, 5th Jan., 1902.	♅ r. 20♐ ♄ r. 21¾♑ ♂ p. 20♓	♇ r. 16¾ ♊ ☉ p. 15♓	☿ r. 2¾ ♓	♀ p. 17½♒ M.C. con. 19¾ ♌	♄ con. 18½♑
Monthly Angles and Planets	Progressed 31st Jan., 1903. Converse, 8th Feb., 1901.		M.C. p. 16♍		☉ con. 18♒	
Weekly Angles and Planets	Progressed 23rd May 1906. Converse, 18th Oct., 1897.	♇ p. 21¾ ♊	♂ p. 17 ♊ ♃ p. 14½ ♊ ♄ p. 14♓ ♇ con. 14¼ ♊	♄ con. 2½♐ ☿ con. 2½ ♊ Asc. con. 5½ ♍		
Daily Angles and Planets	Progressed 1st March, 1932. Converse, 9th Jan., 1872.	♀ p. 21 ♈ ♇ p. 20♋ ♆ con. 21 ♈ Asc. con. 21 ♏		♂ p. 4 ♓ ♆ p. 6½ ♍ M.C. con. 4♍	♂ con. 19♒ ♇ con. 18♉	M.C. p. 17 ♎ ♅ p. 17 ♈ ☉ con. 18½♑

Columns 1, 2 and 3 vividly portray the tragic story while in Column 4 the ominous import of the converse daily Mars square Pluto acquires fresh menace when measured against the progressed yearly Venus. (See also pages 106, 112 and 119.)

CHARLES LINDBERGH, JUNIOR

Kidnapped and murdered, 1st March, 1932.

Series	*Directional Day*	1	2	3
Radical, Progressed and Converse Angles (Yearly)	Progressed, 24th June, 1930.	Asc. r. 17¼ ♎ Asc. p. 18½ ♎ M.C. con. 18¼ ♋	Asc. con. 15¾ ♎	
Radical, Progressed and Converse Planets (Yearly)	Converse, 20th June, 1930.	☿ r. 18½ ♋	♅ r. 15 ♈ ♂ p. 15¾ ♉	♀ r. 4¼ ♌
Monthly Angles and Planets	Progressed, 12th July, 1930. Converse, 2nd June, 1930.	☉ p. 19¼ ♋	☿ p. 15¾ ♋ ♅ p. 15¼ ♈	
Weekly Angles and Planets	Progressed, 18th September, 1930. Converse, 26th March, 1930.	♀ con. 17 ♈	M.C. p. 14½ ♎ ♃ p. 16 ♋ ♂ p. 12½ ♋ ♅ p. 14 ♈	♄ p. 5 ♑ ☉ con. 5 ♈
Daily Angles and Planets	Progressed, 1st March, 1932. Converse, 12th October, 1928.	Asc. p. 18¾ ♋ ♅ p. 17¼ ♈ ☉ con. 18 ♎	♃ p. 14¾ ♌ Asc. con. 13 ♑ ♀ con. 15 ♏ ♄ con. 15 ♐	♅ con. 5 ♈

As the baby was less than two years old relatively few aspects other than those present in the natal chart have had time to develop. Columns 1 and 2 particularly show how acutely the radical afflictions were brought to a head. (See also pages 105, 111 and 118.)

ALBERT EINSTEIN

Friend Dr. Rathenau assassinated, and own life threatened, 24th June, 1922.

Series	*Directional Day*	1	2	3	4	5	6	7	8
Radical, Progressed and Converse Angles (Yearly)	Progressed 26th Apr., 1879.	M.C. con. 1♒	M.C. p. 26¾♈	Asc. con. 28¾♉ Cusp 8r. 29♑	M.C. r. 14¼♓				
Radical, Progressed and Converse Planets (Yearly)	Converse, 30th Jan., 1879.	☊ r. 1½♒ ♅ r. 1½♍	♂ r. 27 ♑ ♂ con. 26♐	♂ p. 28½♒	☽ r. 14½♐	♀ r. 17♈	☉ r. 23½♓	♆ r. 7¾♉	♄ p. 9♈
Monthly Angles and Planets	Progressed 14th Aug., 1880. Converse, 11th Oct., 1877.	♀ p. 0¾♍	♃ con. 27¾♐	♄ p. 29♈ ☊ con. 29♒ ♅ con. 28 ♌ ♀ con. 28♍	♂ p. 15½♍ ♄ con. 14¾ ♓	☉ con. 18¼♎			
Weekly Angles and Planets	Progressed 19th May, 1885. Converse, 6th Jan., 1873.	☿ p. 1½♊ ♃ con. 0¾♍		☉ p. 28½♉ ♅ p. 29♍ ♃ p. 27♌ Asc. p. 28¼♌ ♀ con. 28♒		☉ con. 16½♑ Asc. con. 15½♈	♄ p. 24♊ ☿ con. 23¼♐	♂ p. 8♉	
Daily Angles and Planets	Progressed 24th June, 1922. Converse, 3rd Dec., 1835.	M.C. con. 1¼♐ ♄ con. 1¼♏ ♆ con. 1¾♒	♀ con. 25½♐	♅ con. 27♒ ☊ con. 28¼♌	♅ p. 13½♓ ♂ p. 14½♐ ♆ p. 14♌ ♂ con. 15¼♐ ♃ con. 14½♋ ♀ con. 13♈		☿ p. 23¼♊ M.C. p. 23♊ Asc. p. 24¾♍		♃ p. 9½♎ ♀ p. 9¼♋

The directions in Columns 1, 3 and 4 mark the period as extremely critical.

COLONEL CHARLES LINDBERGH

Flew the Atlantic, 20th May, 1927.

Series	*Directional Day*	1	2	3	4	5	6
Radical, Progressed and Converse Angles (Yearly)	Progressed, 1st Mar., 1902.	M.C. p. 15¾♎ Asc. con. 14♏	Asc. p. 22¼♐	M.C. con. 24¾♌		Asc. r. 3♐	
Radical, Progressed and Converse Planets (Yearly)	Converse, 10th Jan., 1902.	☉ r. 14½♒ ♀ r. 16¾♊	☽ r. 25¾♐ ♅ r. 20¼♐ (mid-point 23♐)		☽ r. 25¾♐ ♂ r. 26¼♒	☿ r. 2¾♓	♆ r. 29♊ ♃ r. 29½♑ ♀ con. 29♒
Monthly Angles and Planets	Progressed, 5th Dec., 1902. Converse, 6th Apr., 1901.	Asc. p. 14 ♎ ♀ p. 14¼♐ ☉ con. 15¾♈ ♄ con. 16♑ ♅ con. 16¾♐	♂ p. 23♍ ♂ con. 23♌		♄ p. 25♑ Asc con 26½♐ ♆ con. 26¾♊		
Weekly Angles and Planets	Progressed, 15th Sept., 1905. Converse, 25th June, 1898.	♂ p. 15♐ ♀ p. 16♌	☉ p. 22♍ ♆ con. 22¾♊		☿ con. 27¾ ♊	☿ p. 4♍ ☉ con. 3¾♋	M.C. p. 28½♈
Daily Angles and Planets	Progressed, 20th May, 1927. Converse, 21st Oct., 1876.			♆ p. 24♌ ♅ con. 24♌ ♀ con. 24♉		♅ p. 2½♈ ♄ p. 4¾♐ Asc. con. 4♊ ♃ con. 3¼♐	☉ p. 28♉ ☿ p. 28¼♉ ☉ con. 28♎

The radical Moon, Mars, Uranus configuration was probably the mainspring of this great achievement. Columns 2, 3 and 4 are therefore closely linked. Columns 1 and 5 also emphasize important radical configurations.

ANNE MORROW LINDBERGH

Married, 27th May, 1929.

Series	*Directional Day*	1	2	3	4	5	6	7
Radical, Progressed and Converse Angles (Yearly)	Progressed, 15th July, 1906.	M.C. p. 20½♋	Asc. p. 17½♎	M.C. r. 28¾♊ Asc. r. 29♍	M.C. con. 6¾♊			
Radical, Progressed and Converse Planets (Yearly)	Converse, 30th May, 1906.			♀ p. 29¾♌	♂ r. 7¼♋	♃ p. 26¾♊	☉ r. 0¼♋	♃ r. 21½♊ ☿ r. 22½♊ ♂ con. 21¾♊ ☉ p. 21½♋
Monthly Angles and Planets	Progressed, 24th March, 1907.	Asc. p. 19¾♋ ♄ p. 19½♓				♂ p. 26♊	M.C. p. 1¼♈	♀ p. 20¼♒ ☿ p. 21½♓
	Converse, 20th Sept., 1905.			☊ con. 28½ ♌	Asc. con. 7¾♐ ♃ con. 6½♊	M.C. con. 25½♍ ☉ con. 27♍	♅ con. 0¼♑	♀ con. 22¼♌
Weekly Angles and Planets	Progressed, 30th Sept., 1909.	♆ p. 19¼♋ ♄ p. 20¾♈	♅ p. 17♑	♂ p. 29♓	☉ p. 6¾♎	♃ p. 27½♍ ☿ p. 26¾♊		
	Converse, 14th March, 1903.		♀ con. 18♈ ☊ con. 17¼♎ ☿ con. 17½♊	☿ con. 29½♒		♅ con. 25½♐	♆ con. 1♋	M.C. con. 21½♓ ☉ con. 22¾♓
Daily Angles and Planets	Progressed, 27th May, 1929.		☿ p. 16¾♋	♆ p. 28¾♌ ♄ p. 28¾♐	☉ p. 5¾♊ ♂ p. 8♌	♃ p. 26¼♉ ♀ p. 26♈		☿ p. 22½♊
	Converse, 17th July, 1883.	Asc. con. 19¾♎ ♅ con. 20¼♍ ♆ con. 20¾♉	♃ con. 16♋		♄ con. 6½♊ ♂ con. 5♊ ♀ con. 7♋		♀ con. 0¾♊	

The directions in Columns 3 and 4 have the greatest bearing on this event. The aspects to the radical and the progressed yearly Jupiter are also significant in view of the hazardous flight to the Orient on which she accompanied her husband directly after the marriage.

CONCLUSION

THE system outlined in the foregoing pages is an attempt to fill the need expressed by many astrologers for a method of directing which not only indicates with accuracy the general nature of the events to be anticipated but which is also reliable in determining the timing of those events within narrow limits. It is also designed as a first step in establishing some sort of uniformity between the multiplicity of directional systems at present in vogue. In a future volume it is hoped to show how some of the same simple fundamental principles of Secondary Directing may be applied to Solar Revolutions and other figures of a similar nature, and to demonstrate how these figures may be used in conjunction with Secondary Directions to the mutual advantage of both systems.

The prime importance of the angles of the birth chart has repeatedly been stressed. It is absolutely necessary that the birth chart should be as accurate in this respect as the most careful rectification can make it. It is useless to expect satisfactory results from Secondary Directions unless the angles of the horoscope under consideration have been carefully checked with reference to past events. Even a "stop-watch timed" birth must not be regarded as above suspicion until one or two major events in the life have occurred either to corroborate or to confound the prevailing angular directions. The Daily Series of progressions will often prove to be of great use in testing the accuracy of the radical angles.

One final point. It may have occurred to readers, as it did to me, when studying the various examples of directions given in Chapters V, VI and VII, that the nature of the event often seemed to derive more strongly from the houses ruled or from the signs or houses occupied, than from the intrinsic nature of the planets themselves. Furthermore, in many cases there appeared to be no appreciable difference in effect between signs and houses. Such a state of affairs may be considered a mixed blessing, for, while making for greater simplicity, it appears to offer the astrologer less chance of elaborating his predictions in great detail. In this respect it is well to remember that progressed aspects, besides providing the individual with new opportunities for soul growth, also denote opportunities for him to "work off" some of his debts to the past. The nature of these debts may be diagnosed in terms of the planets involved, of the houses ruled by them, or of the signs and houses they occupy. Although the comparison of similar progressed aspects occurring in different horoscopes is extremely useful and instructive it is not strictly scientific to anticipate an almost identical event taking place under the same type of progressed aspect in two different charts since no two individuals are evolving along exactly the same lines. Thus it behoves us when predicting always to heed the words of wisdom attributed to Ptolemy, "Judgment must be regulated by thyself as well as by the science, for it is not possible that particular forms of events should be declared by any person, however scientific, since the understanding conceives only a general idea of some sensible event, and not its particular form. It is, therefore, necessary for him who practises herein to adopt inference. They only who are inspired by the Deity can predict particulars."

TABLE 1
The Days of the Year numbered

Conversion Tables for the Calculation of Progressed and Converse Directional Days.

Date	Day Number	Date	Day Number	Date	Day Number	Date	Day Number
Jan. 1	1	Feb. 13	44	Mar. 28	87	May 9	129
" 2	2	" 14	45	" 29	88	" 10	130
" 3	3	" 15	46	" 30	89	" 11	131
" 4	4	" 16	47	" 31	90	" 12	132
" 5	5	" 17	48			" 13	133
" 6	6	" 18	49	Apr. 1	91	" 14	134
" 7	7	" 19	50	" 2	92	" 15	135
" 8	8	" 20	51	" 3	93	" 16	136
" 9	9	" 21	52	" 4	94	" 17	137
" 10	10	" 22	53	" 5	95	" 18	138
" 11	11	" 23	54	" 6	96	" 19	139
" 12	12	" 24	55	" 7	97	" 20	140
" 13	13	" 25	56	" 8	98	" 21	141
" 14	14	" 26	57	" 9	99	" 22	142
" 15	15	" 27	58	" 10	100	" 23	143
" 16	16	" 28	59	" 11	101	" 24	144
" 17	17			" 12	102	" 25	145
" 18	18	Mar. 1	60	" 13	103	" 26	146
" 19	19	" 2	61	" 14	104	" 27	147
" 20	20	" 3	62	" 15	105	" 28	148
" 21	21	" 4	63	" 16	106	" 29	149
" 22	22	" 5	64	" 17	107	" 30	150
" 23	23	" 6	65	" 18	108	" 31	151
" 24	24	" 7	66	" 19	109		
" 25	25	" 8	67	" 20	110	June 1	152
" 26	26	" 9	68	" 21	111	" 2	153
" 27	27	" 10	69	" 22	112	" 3	154
" 28	28	" 11	70	" 23	113	" 4	155
" 29	29	" 12	71	" 24	114	" 5	156
" 30	30	" 13	72	" 25	115	" 6	157
" 31	31	" 14	73	" 26	116	" 7	158
		" 15	74	" 27	117	" 8	159
Feb. 1	32	" 16	75	" 28	118	" 9	160
" 2	33	" 17	76	" 29	119	" 10	161
" 3	34	" 18	77	" 30	120	" 11	162
" 4	35	" 19	78			" 12	163
" 5	36	" 20	79	May 1	121	" 13	164
" 6	37	" 21	80	" 2	122	" 14	165
" 7	38	" 22	81	" 3	123	" 15	166
" 8	39	" 23	82	" 4	124	" 16	167
" 9	40	" 24	83	" 5	125	" 17	168
" 10	41	" 25	84	" 6	126	" 18	169
" 11	42	" 26	85	" 7	127	" 19	170
" 12	43	" 27	86	" 8	128	" 20	171

Date	Day Number	Date	Day Number	Date	Day Number	Date	Day Number
June 21	172	Aug. 13	225	Oct. 5	278	Nov. 28	332
,, 22	173	,, 14	226	,, 6	279	,, 29	333
,, 23	174	,, 15	227	,, 7	280	,, 30	334
,, 24	175	,, 16	228	,, 8	281	Dec. 1	335
,, 25	176	,, 17	229	,, 9	282	,, 2	336
,, 26	177	,, 18	230	,, 10	283	,, 3	337
,, 27	178	,, 19	231	,, 11	284	,, 4	338
,, 28	179	,, 20	232	,, 12	285	,, 5	339
,, 29	180	,, 21	233	,, 13	286	,, 6	340
,, 30	181	,, 22	234	,, 14	287	,, 7	341
July 1	182	,, 23	235	,, 15	288	,, 8	342
,, 2	183	,, 24	236	,, 16	289	,, 9	343
,, 3	184	,, 25	237	,, 17	290	,, 10	344
,, 4	185	,, 26	238	,, 18	291	,, 11	345
,, 5	186	,, 27	239	,, 19	292	,, 12	346
,, 6	187	,, 28	240	,, 20	293	,, 13	347
,, 7	188	,, 29	241	,, 21	294	,, 14	348
,, 8	189	,, 30	242	,, 22	295	,, 15	349
,, 9	190	,, 31	243	,, 23	296	,, 16	350
,, 10	191	Sept. 1	244	,, 24	297	,, 17	351
,, 11	192	,, 2	245	,, 25	298	,, 18	352
,, 12	193	,, 3	246	,, 26	299	,, 19	353
,, 13	194	,, 4	247	,, 27	300	,, 20	354
,, 14	195	,, 5	248	,, 28	301	,, 21	355
,, 15	196	,, 6	249	,, 29	302	,, 22	356
,, 16	197	,, 7	250	,, 30	303	,, 23	357
,, 17	198	,, 8	251	,, 31	304	,, 24	358
,, 18	199	,, 9	252	Nov. 1	305	,, 25	359
,, 19	200	,, 10	253	,, 2	306	,, 26	360
,, 20	201	,, 11	254	,, 3	307	,, 27	361
,, 21	202	,, 12	255	,, 4	308	,, 28	362
,, 22	203	,, 13	256	,, 5	309	,, 29	363
,, 23	204	,, 14	257	,, 6	310	,, 30	364
,, 24	205	,, 15	258	,, 7	311	,, 31	365
,, 25	206	,, 16	259	,, 8	312		
,, 26	207	,, 17	260	,, 9	313		
,, 27	208	,, 18	261	,, 10	314		
,, 28	209	,, 19	262	,, 11	315		
,, 29	210	,, 20	263	,, 12	316		
,, 30	211	,, 21	264	,, 13	317		
,, 31	212	,, 22	265	,, 14	318		
Aug. 1	213	,, 23	266	,, 15	319		
,, 2	214	,, 24	267	,, 16	320		
,, 3	215	,, 25	268	,, 17	321		
,, 4	216	,, 26	269	,, 18	322		
,, 5	217	,, 27	270	,, 19	323		
,, 6	218	,, 28	271	,, 20	324		
,, 7	219	,, 29	272	,, 21	325		
,, 8	220	,, 30	273	,, 22	326		
,, 9	221	Oct. 1	274	,, 23	327		
,, 10	222	,, 2	275	,, 24	328		
,, 11	223	,, 3	276	,, 25	329		
,, 12	224	,, 4	277	,, 26	330		
				,, 27	331		

To find the converse daily directional day by means of Table 1:—

1. Find in the Table the number of the day for which it is desired to calculate the equivalent date before birth.

2. Subtract from this number the number of the day of birth. (If the second number is greater than the first, add 365 to the first number.)

3. Calculate the native's age in years on the birthday preceding the day for which the equivalent directional day before birth is being determined.

4. Count the number of Leap Year Days falling in the period between the day of birth and the day for which the directional day is being determined.

5. Subtract the number obtained as a result of operation 2 from the number of the day of birth. (If the first number is greater than the second, add 365 to it.)

6. Find in the Table the day of the year corresponding to the number found by operation 5.

7. Subtract the number of years obtained by operation 3 from the birth year. (If it has been necessary to add 365 before the subtraction in operation 5 could be made, deduct a further year from the birth year.) This will give the year in which the converse daily directional day will fall.

One final adjustment may be necessary!

8. Count the number of Leap Year Days falling between the directional day so found and the day of birth. Subtract from this number the number obtained under operation 4. If there is no remainder the directional day as calculated above will need no adjustment. If the remainder is a *positive* number, it will be necessary to make the directional day *later* by that number of days. If the remainder is a *negative* number it will be necessary to make the directional day *earlier* by that number of days.

EXAMPLE CALCULATION

It is required to find the converse daily directional day measuring to 17th January, 1937, in the life of Ann Harding. The procedure is as follows:—

Date for which converse daily directional day is required....17th January, 1937.

Date of Birth...7th August, 1902.

Age of native on 17th January, 1937..........................34 years 163 days

Subtract 34 years from 1902.. 1868

Day number of 7th August (see Table 1) 219

Subtract 163 days...56
$$= \text{25th February, 1868}$$

To see whether any adjustment needs to be made to this date:—

Count the number of Leap Year days† occurring between 7th August, 1902, and 17th January, 1937 9

Count the number of Leap Year days† occurring between 7th August, 1902, and 25th February, 1868 8

Number of Leap Year days less in period before birth............................1
.·. Directional day must be one day earlier = 24th February, 1868.

---

* Had this number been less than 164, it would have been necessary to have added 365 to it, afterwards subtracting one more year from the year of birth.

† A list of Leap Years is given in Table 4.

TABLE 2

To convert years into days at the rate of a day for a month

Column 1	Column 2		Column 1	Column 2		Column 1	Column 2	
Age	Equivalent number of years and days		Age	Equivalent number of years and days		Age	Equivalent number of years and days	
Years	Years	Days	Years	Years	Days	Years	Years	Days
1	—	12	31	1	7	61	2	2
2	—	24	32	1	19	62	2	14
3	—	36	33	1	31	63	2	26
4	—	48	34	1	43	64	2	38
5	—	60	35	1	55	65	2	50
6	—	72	36	1	67	66	2	62
7	—	84	37	1	79	67	2	74
8	—	96	38	1	91	68	2	86
9	—	108	39	1	103	69	2	98
10	—	120	40	1	115	70	2	110
11	—	132	41	1	127	71	2	122
12	—	144	42	1	139	72	2	134
13	—	156	43	1	151	73	2	146
14	—	168	44	1	163	74	2	158
15	—	180	45	1	175	75	2	170
16	—	192	46	1	187	76	2	182
17	—	204	47	1	199	77	2	194
18	—	216	48	1	211	78	2	206
19	—	228	49	1	223	79	2	218
20	—	240	50	1	235	80	2	230
21	—	252	51	1	247	81	2	242
22	—	264	52	1	259	82	2	254
23	—	276	53	1	271	83	2	266
24	—	288	54	1	283	84	2	278
25	—	300	55	1	295	85	2	290
26	—	312	56	1	307	86	2	302
27	—	324	57	1	319	87	2	314
28	—	336	58	1	331	88	2	326
29	—	348	59	1	343	89	2	338
30	—	360	60	1	355	90	2	350

To find the progressed and converse monthly directional days by means of Tables 1 and 2:—

1. Calculate the native's age in years measuring to the period under review.

2. Using Conversion Table 2, find this figure in Column 1 and note the number of days and years opposite to it in Column 2. This number represents the number of years and days before and after birth measuring to the required period.

If the period elapsed since birth is more than an exact number of years, calculate the number of months in the remaining period and for each month add an extra day to the number obtained above.

3. Turn to Table 1 and note the number opposite the native's day of birth. To find the progressed monthly directional day add to this number the number of days obtained as a result of operation 2 above. (If the number so found is in excess of 365, subtract 365 from it.)

4. Find, in Table 1, the date which is opposite this new number. This date will be the required progressed monthly directional day. If the native is more than thirty years and five months old, add on the "year" figure also to the year of birth. If, in operation 3, it was found necessary to subtract 365, add one more year, whatever the native's age.

Be careful to allow for any Leap Year Day falling in the period between the day of birth and the progressed monthly directional day. For every such day it will be necessary to make the directional day one day earlier than that shown in the table.

5. To find the converse monthly directional day subtract from the day of birth number the number of days obtained as a result of operation 2 above. (If the first number is less than the second, add 365 to it.)

6. Find in Table 1 the date opposite the number obtained as a result of operation 5. This date will be the required converse monthly directional day. If the native is more than thirty years and five months old, subtract the year figure from the year of birth. If in operation 5, it was found necessary to add 365, deduct one more year, whatever the natives' age.

Be careful to allow for any Leap Year Day falling in the period between the day of birth and the converse monthly directional day. For every such day it will be necessary to make the directional day one day later than that shown in the table.

EXAMPLE CALCULATION

It is required to find the progressed and converse monthly directional days measuring to 17th January, 1937, in the life of Ann Harding. The procedure is as follows:—

Date for which directional days required......................17th January, 1937

Date of birth ....7th August, 1902

Age of native on 17th January, 1937..........................34 years 5 months

Equivalent number of days for 34 years.........................1 year 43 days

Add equivalent number of days for 5 months....................1 year 48 days

Day number of 7th August (see Table 1)...............................219

To obtain progressed monthly directional day add...........................48
                                                                        ———
Day number of directional day...267
                                                                        ———
                                                          = 24th September

Add 1 year to year of birth...1903

Progressed monthly directional day....................24th September[1], 1903

To obtain the converse monthly directional day:—

From the day number for 7th August...................................219

Subtract 48
                                                                        ———
Day number of directional day 171
                                                                        ———
                                                              = 20th June

Subtract 1 year from year of birth...................................1901

Converse monthly directional day .... 20th June[2], 1901

---
[1] Had 1903 been a Leap Year it would have been necessary to have made the directional day one day earlier
[2] Had 1902 been a Leap Year it would have been necessary to have made the directional day one day later

TABLE 3
To convert years into days at the rate of a day for a week

N.B.—The normal year of 365 days does not divide exactly into 52 weeks, there being one day over. Leap Years, of course, have two days over. These "extra" days are listed cumulatively in Column 1 until they total seven, when they are cancelled out by the addition of one day in Column 2. It is necessary to take these odd days into account when computing the number of weeks in a period of less than a year.

The table is drawn up as if the twelve months immediately prior to birth contained a Leap Year Day. Subsequent Leap Year Days therefore fall during the fourth, eighth, and twelfth years and so on throughout the life. In cases where the Leap Years fall differently

Column 1 — Age		Column 2 — Equivalent number of years and days		Column 1 — Age		Column 2 — Equivalent number of years and days		Column 1 — Age		Column 2 — Equivalent number of years and days	
Years	Days	Years	Days	Years	Days	Years	Days	Years	Days	Years	Days
1	1	—	52	31	3	4	156	61	6	8	260
2	2	—	104	32	5	4	208	62	—	8	313
3	3	—	156	33	6	4	260	63	1	9	—
4	5	—	208	34	—	4	313	64	3	9	52
5	6	—	260	35	1	5	—	65	4	9	104
6	—	—	313	36	3	5	52	66	5	9	156
7	1	1	—	37	4	5	104	67	6	9	208
8	3	1	52	38	5	5	156	68	1	9	261
9	4	1	104	39	6	5	208	69	2	9	313
10	5	1	156	40	1	5	261	70	3	10	—
11	6	1	208	41	2	5	313	71	4	10	52
12	1	1	261	42	3	6	—	72	6	10	104
13	2	1	313	43	4	6	52	73	—	10	157
14	3	2	—	44	6	6	104	74	1	10	209
15	4	2	52	45	—	6	157	75	2	10	261
16	6	2	104	46	1	6	209	76	4	10	313
17	—	2	157	47	2	6	261	77	5	11	—
18	1	2	209	48	4	6	313	78	6	11	52
19	2	2	261	49	5	7	—	79	—	11	105
20	4	2	313	50	6	7	52	80	2	11	157
21	5	3	—	51	—	7	105	81	3	11	209
22	6	3	52	52	2	7	157	82	4	11	261
23	—	3	105	53	3	7	209	83	5	11	313
24	2	3	157	54	4	7	261	84	—	12	—
25	3	3	209	55	5	7	313	85	1	12	52
26	4	3	261	56	—	8	—	86	2	12	104
27	5	3	313	57	1	8	52	87	3	12	156
28	—	4	—	58	2	8	104	88	5	12	208
29	1	4	52	59	3	8	156	89	6	12	260
30	2	4	104	60	5	8	208	90	—	12	313

it is necessary to make the following adjustments to Column 2 of the table:—

1. When Leap Year Day falls during the first year of life:—

(a) To directional periods equivalent to 5, 33, 61 and 89 years—add 1 day.

(*b*) From directional periods equivalent to 8–10, 12–21, 23–27, 36–38, 40–49, 51–55, 64–66, 68–77 and 79–83 years—*subtract* 1 day.

(*c*) For directional periods equivalent to 7, 35 and 63 years—*substitute* 365 days, 4 years 365 days and 8 years 365 days respectively.

(*d*) The remaining directional periods need no adjustment.

(*e*) The sequence of the "extra" days in Column 1 will be the same as that beginning at age 24.

2. When Leap Year Day falls during the second year of life:—

(*a*) To directional periods equivalent to 11, 39 and 67 years—*add* 1 day.

(*b*) From directional periods equivalent to 15–21, 23–27, 43–49, 51–55, 71–77 and 79–83 years—*subtract* 1 day.

(*c*) For directional periods equivalent to 14, 42 and 70 years—*substitute* 1 year 365 days, 5 years 365 days and 9 years 365 days respectively.

(*d*) The remaining directional periods need no adjustment.

(*e*) The sequence of "extra" days in Column 1 will be the same as that beginning at age 7.

3. When Leap Year Day falls during the third year of life:—

(*a*) To directional periods equivalent to 11, 39 and 67 years—*add* 1 day.

(*b*) From directional periods equivalent to 22–27, 50–55 and 78–83 years—*deduct* 1 day.

(*c*) For directional periods equivalent to 21, 49 and 77 years—*substitute* 2 years 365 days, 6 years 365 days and 10 years 365 days, respectively.

(*d*) The remaining directional periods need no adjustment.

(*e*) The sequence of "extra" days in Column 1 will be the same as that beginning at age 18.

N.B.—(1) Remember that if the native was born less than twelve months after Leap Year Day, Table 3 is only suitable, as it stands, for the calculation of *progressed* directions. Leap Year Day will fall in the *first* year *before* birth and consequently, for the calculation of converse directions, the adjustments in variation 1 above must be applied. Similarly, if variation 2 is appropriate for progressed directions, variation 3 must be used for converse directions, and so on.

(2) This table does not allow for the fact that 1900 was not a Leap Year. Therefore, to all directional periods which include this year, it will be necessary to *add* one day. It will also be necessary to *deduct* one day from the "extra" days in column 1 according to the native's age (measured forwards or backwards) in the year 1900.

To find the progressed and converse weekly directional days by means of Tables 1 and 3:—

1. Calculate the native's age in years measuring to the period under review.

2. Using Conversion Table 3, find this figure in Column 1 and note the number of years and days opposite to it in Column 2. This will be the number of years and days before and after birth measuring to the required period.

If the required period exceeds an exact number of years, calculate the number of weeks over and for each week add a day to the directional period obtained above.

3. Turn to Table 1 and note the number opposite the native's day of birth. To find the progressed weekly directional day add to this number the number of days obtained

as a result of operation 2 above. (If the number so found is in excess of 365, subtract 365 from it.)

4. Find, in Table 1, the date which is opposite this new number. This date will be the required progressed weekly directional day. If the native is over seven years old, add on the "year" figure to the year of birth. If, in operation 3, it was found necessary to subtract 365, add one more year, whatever the native's age.

5. To find the converse weekly directional day subtract from the day of birth number the number of days obtained as a result of operation 2 above. (If the first number is less than the second, add 365 to it.)

6. Find, in Table 1, the date opposite the number obtained as a result of operation 5. This date will be the required converse weekly directional day. If the native is more than seven years old, subtract the year figure from the year of birth. If, in operation 5, it was found necessary to add 365, deduct one more year, whatever the native's age.

EXAMPLE CALCULATION

It is required to find the progressed and converse weekly directional days measuring to 17th January, 1937, in the life of Ann Harding. The procedure is as follows:—

Date for which directional days required........................17th January, 1937

Date of birth ....7th August, 1902

Age of native on 17th January, 1937..........................34 years 163 days

Add to "days" figure number of days excess for 34 years (1)* from Column 1 (Table 3) .... 164 days

Turn into weeks ....23 weeks

Equivalent number of days for 34 years (see Table 3)...............4 years 313 days

Add equivalent number of days for 23 weeks........................4 years 336 days

Day number of 7th August (see Table 1) 219

To obtain progressed weekly directional day add.............................336

                                                                            555
Subtract 365 365

Day number of directional day...190

                                                                    = 9th July
Add 5 years to the year of birth (includes 1 year extra for 365 subtraction)........1907

Progressed weekly directional day..............................9th July, 1907

To obtain the converse weekly directional day:—

From the day number for 7th August......................................219

* Table adjusted as Leap Year Day falls in second year of life. (See 2(e) above.)

Subtract ....·337*

Add 365 to 219 ....·584

Day number of directional day (584—337)·······························.247

= 4th September

Subtract 5 years from the date of birth (includes 1 year extra for 365 addition)....1897

Converse weekly directional day ....4th September, 1897

TABLE 4
List of Leap Years

The following are the Leap Years in the nineteenth and twentieth centuries. Only the last two figures of the year are given as the Leap Years in the two centuries are interchangeable in so far as these two figures are concerned.

04	24	44	64	84
08	28	48	68	88
12	32	52	72	92
16	36	56	76	96
20	40	60	80	

* Figure adjusted as the directional period contains the year 1900, which was not a Leap Year.

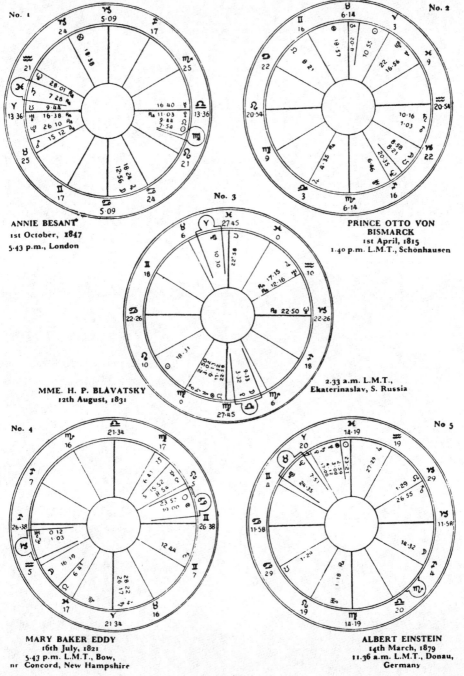

ANNIE BESANT
1st October, 1847
5·43 p.m., London

**PRINCE OTTO VON
BISMARCK**
1st April, 1815
1.40 p.m. L.M.T., Schonhausen

MME. H. P. BLAVATSKY
12th August, 1831

2.33 a.m. L.M.T.,
Ekaterinaslav, S. Russia

MARY BAKER EDDY
16th July, 1821
5·43 p.m. L.M.T., Bow,
nr Concord, New Hampshire

ALBERT EINSTEIN
14th March, 1879
11.36 a.m. L.M.T., Donau,
Germany

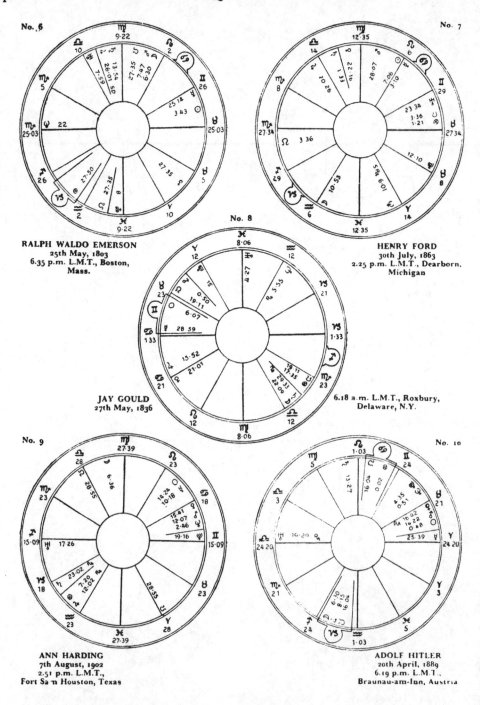

RALPH WALDO EMERSON
25th May, 1803
6.35 p.m. L.M.T., Boston,
Mass.

HENRY FORD
30th July, 1863
2.25 p.m. L.M.T., Dearborn,
Michigan

JAY GOULD
27th May, 1836

6.18 a.m. L.M.T., Roxbury,
Delaware, N.Y.

ANN HARDING
7th August, 1902
2.51 p.m. L.M.T.,
Fort Sam Houston, Texas

ADOLF HITLER
20th April, 1889
6.19 p.m. L.M.T.,
Braunau-am-Inn, Austria

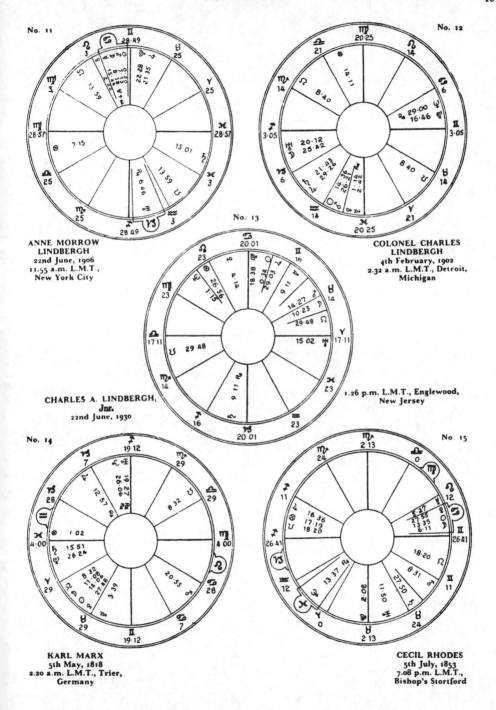

No. 11

ANNE MORROW
LINDBERGH
22nd June, 1906
11.55 a.m. L.M.T.,
New York City

No. 12

COLONEL CHARLES
LINDBERGH
4th February, 1902
2.32 a.m. L.M.T., Detroit,
Michigan

No. 13

CHARLES A. LINDBERGH,
Jnr.
22nd June, 1930

1.26 p.m. L.M.T., Englewood,
New Jersey

No. 14

KARL MARX
5th May, 1818
2.20 a.m. L.M.T., Trier,
Germany

No. 15

CECIL RHODES
5th July, 1853
7.08 p.m. L.M.T.,
Bishop's Stortford

INDEX